An Introduction to
Duplicate Detection

Synthesis Lectures on Data Management

Editor
M. Tamer Özsu, *University of Waterloo*

Synthesis Lectures on Data Management is edited by Tamer Özsu of the University of Waterloo. The series will publish 50- to 125 page publications on topics pertaining to data management. The scope will largely follow the purview of premier information and computer science conferences, such as ACM SIGMOD, VLDB, ICDE, PODS, ICDT, and ACM KDD. Potential topics include, but they are not limited to the following: query languages, database system architectures, transaction management, data warehousing, XML and databases, data stream systems, wide scale data distribution, multimedia data management, data mining, and related subjects.

An Introduction to Duplicate Detection
Felix Naumann and Melanie Herschel
2010

Privacy-Preserving Data Publishing: An Overview
Raymond Chi-Wing Wong and Ada Wai-Chee Fu
2010

Keyword Search in Databases
Jeffrey Xu Yu, Lu Qin, and Lijun Chang
2009

An Introduction to Duplicate Detection

Felix Naumann and Melanie Herschel

ISBN: 978-3-031-00707-1   paperback
ISBN: 978-3-031-01835-0   ebook

DOI 10.1007/978-3-031-01835-0

A Publication in the Springer series
SYNTHESIS LECTURES ON DATA MANAGEMENT

Lecture #3
Series Editor: M. Tamer Özsu, *University of Waterloo*
Series ISSN
Synthesis Lectures on Data Management
Print 2153-5418   Electronic 2153-5426

An Introduction to Duplicate Detection

Felix Naumann
Hasso Plattner Institute, Potsdam

Melanie Herschel
University of Tübingen

SYNTHESIS LECTURES ON DATA MANAGEMENT #3

ABSTRACT

With the ever increasing volume of data, data quality problems abound. Multiple, yet different representations of the same real-world objects in data, duplicates, are one of the most intriguing data quality problems. The effects of such duplicates are detrimental; for instance, bank customers can obtain duplicate identities, inventory levels are monitored incorrectly, catalogs are mailed multiple times to the same household, etc.

Automatically detecting duplicates is difficult: First, duplicate representations are usually not identical but slightly differ in their values. Second, in principle all pairs of records should be compared, which is infeasible for large volumes of data. This lecture examines closely the two main components to overcome these difficulties: (i) Similarity measures are used to automatically identify duplicates when comparing two records. Well-chosen similarity measures improve the *effectiveness* of duplicate detection. (ii) Algorithms are developed to perform on very large volumes of data in search for duplicates. Well-designed algorithms improve the *efficiency* of duplicate detection. Finally, we discuss methods to evaluate the success of duplicate detection.

KEYWORDS

data quality, data cleansing, data cleaning, ETL, similarity measures, entity matching, object matching, record linkage

Contents

CHAPTER 1

Data Cleansing: Introduction and Motivation

With the ever increasing volume of data and the ever improving ability of information systems to gather data from many, distributed, and heterogeneous sources, data quality problems abound. One of the most intriguing data quality problems is that of multiple, yet different representations of the same real-world object in the data. For instance, an individual might be represented multiple times in a customer database, a single product might be listed many times in an online catalog, and data about a single type protein might be stored in many different scientific databases.

Such so-called duplicates are difficult to detect, especially in large volumes of data. Simultaneously, they decrease the usability of the data, cause unnecessary expenses, customer dissatisfaction, incorrect performance indicators, and they inhibit comprehension of the data and its value. Note that duplicates in the context of this lecture are not exact replicas but exhibit slight or even large differences in the individual data values. Thus, such duplicates are also called fuzzy duplicates. In the traditional context of database management systems, duplicates are exact copies of records. They are easy to detect, simply by sorting the data by all columns, and they are thus not topic of this book: We use the term duplicate to refer to fuzzy duplicates. In Table 1.1, records r_1 and r_2 are exact duplicates while r_3 is a fuzzy duplicate with either r_1 or r_2, probably representing the same real-world object.

	FN	LN	Phone	email
r_1	John	Doe	(407) 356 8888	john@doe.com
r_2	John	Doe	(407) 356 8888	john@doe.com
r_3	Jon	Doe	(407) 356 8887	john@doe.com

Table 1.1: Exact duplicate r_1 and r_2 and fuzzy duplicate r_1 and r_3

Duplicates in databases of organizations have many detrimental effects, for instance:

• Fraudulent bank customers can obtain duplicate identities, thus possibly receiving more credit.

• Inventory levels are monitored incorrectly if duplicate products are not recognized. In such cases, the same products are restocked in separate orders, and quantity discounts cannot be gained.

- The total revenue of preferred customers is unknown because it is spread over multiple instances. Gold customers are not recognized and are dissatisfied.

- Catalogs are mailed multiple times to the same household. "Householding" is a special case of person duplicate detection where it is not the same person but persons from the same household who are recognized.

- Duplicate data causes so much more unnecessary IT expenses, simply due to its volume that must be maintained and backed up.

Both researchers and developers in industry have tackled this problem for many decades. It was first examined in 1969 [Fellegi and Sunter, 1969] and has since spawned many research projects and software products. Methods for duplicate detection are included in almost every data warehouse and ETL suite and have reached such mundane places as Microsoft Outlook's contacts-database. In this lecture, we motivate and formally define the problem of duplicate detection. We examine closely the two main components towards its solution: (i) Similarity measures are used to automatically identify duplicates when comparing two records. Well-chosen similarity measures improve the *effectiveness* of duplicate detection. (ii) Algorithms are developed to perform on very large volumes of data in search for duplicates. Well-design algorithms improve the *efficiency* of duplicate detection. Finally, we discuss methods to evaluate the success of duplicate detection.

Figure 1.1 shows a typical duplicate detection process. A set of records R is suspected to contain duplicates. Conceptually, the cross-product of all records is formed, and among those, an algorithm chooses promising candidate pairs, usually those that have a sufficiently high similarity at first glance. These record pairs are then input to a similarity measure, which produces a more sophistically calculated similarity. Finally, similarity thresholds are used to decide whether the pair is indeed a duplicate or not. In some cases, an automated decision is not possible and human expert must inspect the pair in question. One of the goals of duplicate detection is to minimize this set of unsure duplicates without compromising the quality of the overall result.

A slightly different scenario is that of *entity search*. There, it is not the goal to rid a large dataset of duplicates but rather to insert new records into a dataset without producing new duplicates. For instance, customer support specialists solicit name and address of a customer via phone and must be able to immediately recognize whether this customer is already represented in the database. The two scenarios are sometimes distinguished as batch duplicate detection vs. duplicate search or as offline and online duplicate detection. Because of the largely differing requirements, relevant techniques differ, and the topic of entity search warrants a separate lecture. Thus, it is not covered in this lecture.

An obvious next step after detecting duplicates is to combine or merge them and thus produce a single, possibly more complete representation of that real-world object. During this step, possible data conflicts among the multiple representations must somehow be resolved. This second step is called *data fusion* and is not covered in this lecture. Instead, we refer to a survey on data fusion [Bleiholder and Naumann, 2008]. An alternative approach to handle duplicates after their discovery is to somehow link them, thus representing their duplicate status without actually fusing their data.

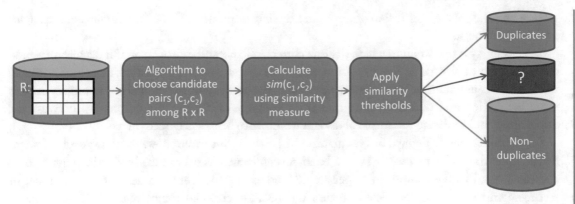

Figure 1.1: A prototypical duplicate detection process

The process of duplicate detection is usually embedded in the more broadly defined process of data cleansing, which not only removes duplicates but performs various other steps, such as address normalization or constraint verification, to improve the overall data quality. In the sections of this chapter, we give an overview of this field of data quality beyond duplicates. We then motivate many causes for inadvertent duplicate creations. Finally, we present several use cases to display the various areas in which duplicate detection plays an important role in an overall information management environment.

1.1   DATA QUALITY

Information and data quality are wide and active research and development areas, both from an information system and a database perspective. They are used synonymously. Broadly, data quality is defined by Tayi and Ballou [1998] as "fitness for use", which is usually broken down into a set of quality dimensions. An in-depth coverage of the topic is given in the book by Batini and Scannapieco [2006]. Here we briefly cover the main issues of data quality with a particular focus of duplicates. First, we mention several pertinent quality dimensions and then cover various aspects of data cleansing, which are usually performed before duplicate detection.

1.1.1   DATA QUALITY DIMENSIONS

In their seminal paper, Wang and Strong [1996] elicit fifteen quality dimensions from questionnaires given to data consumers in the industry; many other classifications are discussed by Batini and Scannapieco [2006]. These widely cited dimensions are categorized as intrinsic (believability, accuracy, objectivity, reputation), contextual (value-added, relevancy, timeliness, completeness, appropriate amount of data), representational (interpretability, ease of understanding, representational consistency, concise representation), and accessibility (accessibility, access security). Obviously, some of the dimensions are highly subjective, and others are not related to duplicates. Duplicate detection and the subsequent fusion of duplicates directly improve quality in the dimensions accuracy and completeness.

Accuracy is the extent to which data are correct, reliable and free of error. It is usually measured as the number of records with errors compared to the overall number of records. Accuracy is usually improved because multiple but different representations of the same real-world object usually implies some conflicting and thus inaccurate data in at least one of the representations – otherwise, the duplicate would have had identical values and would have been easily recognized.

Completeness is defined by Naumann et al. [2004] as the extent to which data are of sufficient depth, breadth and scope for the task at hand. Completeness is often sub-divided into intensional completeness, i.e., the completeness per record, and extensional completeness, i.e., the number or records compared to the complete domain. In general, intensional completeness can be improved through duplicate detection because, in many cases, the multiple representations cover data from different properties; one customer entry might contain a phone number, another entry about the same individual might contain an email address. The combined data are more complete.

Almost all other dimensions are indirectly improved if duplicates are handled appropriately by the information management system. For instance, believability is enhanced because users can assume that a given particular record is the only record about that entity.

1.1.2   DATA CLEANSING

A concrete measure to improve quality of data is to directly modify the data by correcting errors and inconsistencies. Data cleansing[1] is a complex set of tasks that takes as input one or more sets of data and produces as output a single, clean data set. Data cleansing tasks include look-up checks, format transformations, currency conversions, constraint verification, deduplication, data fusion, and many others.

A prominent paradigm for data cleansing is the Extract-Transform-Load (ETL) process, usually built to populate a data warehouse: The extraction phase is responsible for gathering source data and placing it into a so-called staging area. The staging area is usually a relational database system that supports various data cleansing steps. These are performed sequentially or in parallel in the transformation stage. Finally, the load phase is responsible for loading the extracted and cleansed data into the data warehouse / data cube. Figure 1.2 shows a prototypical ETL process with its individual phases and several data cleansing steps. The names of the individual operators have been chosen to reflect typical labels used in ETL products. In the process, two extractors gather data from different sources. A cleansing step specific to one source is performed. Next, a funnel step builds the union of the two sources. A lookup is performed for records with missing zip code data. The match operator performs duplicate detection; the survive operator performs data fusion. Finally, a load operator populates the customer dimension of the data warehouse.

Figure 1.2 is a rather simple process; larger organizations often manage hundreds of more complex ETL processes, which need to be created, maintained, scheduled, and efficiently executed

---

[1]Data cleaning and data cleansing are used synonymously in the literature.

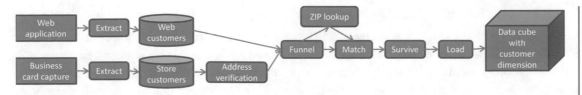

Figure 1.2: A prototypical ETL process

[Albrecht and Naumann, 2008]. ETL engines specialize in efficient, usually parallel execution during times of low load on the transactional system.

Most cleansing tasks are very efficient because they can be executed in a pipeline; therefore, each record can be cleansed individually. For instance, conversions of data values from one measure to another (inch to cm; $ to E) or transforming phone numbers or dates to a standard pattern can be performed independently of other values in that column. Such steps are often referred to as data scrubbing. The intrinsic efficiency of data scrubbing operations is not true for duplicate detection. In principle, each record must be compared to all other records in order to find all duplicates. Chapter 4 describes techniques to avoid this quadratic complexity, but a simple record-by-record approach is not applicable.

Data cleansing is an important pre-processing step before duplicate detection. The more effort is expended here and the cleaner the data become, the better duplicate detection can perform. For instance, a typical standardization is to abbreviate all occurrences of the term "*Street*" in an address column to "*St.*". Thus, the addresses "*20 Main Street*" and "*20 Main St.*" appear as identical strings after standardization. Without standardization, duplicate detection would have to allow for slight deviations to still capture the duplicity of the two addresses. However, this allowance of deviation might already be too loose: "*20 Main St.*" and "*20 Maine St.*" could incorrectly be recognized as the same.

1.2   CAUSES FOR DUPLICATES

One can distinguish two main causes for duplicates in data. First, data about a single entity might be inadvertently entered multiple times into the same database – we call such duplicates *intra-source duplicates*. Second, duplicates appear when integrating multiple data sources, each of which might have a different representation of a single entity – we call such duplicates *inter-source duplicates*.

While the causes for duplicates might differ, methods to detect them are largely the same. What again differs is the treatment of the duplicates once they are discovered: Intra-source duplicates usually undergo some data fusion process to produce a new and enhanced single representation. Inter-source duplicates, on the other hand, are usually merely annotated as such. Combining them is then left to the application that uses the data.

1.2.1   INTRA-SOURCE DUPLICATES

Duplicates within a single data source usually appear when data about an entity are entered without (properly) checking for existing representations of that entity. A typical case is when a customer calls in a new order. While entering the customer data, the system or the clerk does not recognize that this customer is already represented in the database. This can happen due to poor online duplicate detection methods or because of significant changes in the customer data – new last name, new address, etc. Other sources of error are poor data entry: even if the customer data are unchanged, it is entered differently. Causes are, for instance,

- inadvertent typos: 1969 vs. 1996, Felix vs. FElix

- misheard words: Mohammed vs. Mohammad

- difficult names: Britney vs. Britny, Spears vs. Speers, or Vaithyanathan.

- lacking spelling abilities: Philadelfia

Apart from actually incorrect errors, other causes of errors and thus of duplicates are different conventions and data entry formats. This is especially a problem when users, rather than trained data entry clerks, enter their data themselves, as is the case with many online shopping portals and other points of registration on the Web. Figure 1.3 shows five conference name tags with members from the same institute. On the conference registration site, each participant entered his or her own data. While the names and affiliations are all correct, it is not trivial for a computer to decide whether their affiliations are all the same.

Figure 1.3: Five different representations of the same conference attendee affiliation

A typical non-human source of error is the automated scanning of paper documents. Even though this optical character recognition (OCR) technology is very advanced and considered solved for non-cursive machine- and handwriting, not all hand-written or printed documents have the necessary quality. Figure 1.4 shows an example of an incorrect scan. While letters with both addresses are likely to arrive at the correct, same destination, it would be difficult to trace the letter: A database search for the correct name and address would probably not produce that shipment.

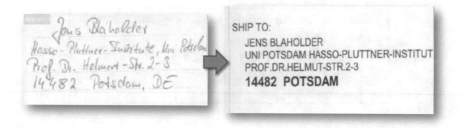

Figure 1.4: Erroneous character recognition for Jens Bleiholder of the Hasso Plattner Institute

1.2.2   INTER-SOURCE DUPLICATES

The problems mentioned above with respect to data entry are also valid for inter-source duplicates. When data about a single individual are entered differently in each source, they constitute a duplicate when the sources are integrated. However, when integrating data sources, there are yet more causes for duplicates:

Different data entry requirements. Even when entering the same information about a real-world object, different sources might have different data entry requirements. For instance, one source might allow abbreviated first names while the other enters the full first name. Titles of a person might be entered in front of the first or in front of the last name. Numerical values might be recorded at different precision levels, data might be entered in different languages, etc. All these are reasons that semantically same information is represented differently. These differences are difficult to specify, making duplicate detection a challenging problem.

Different data entry times. Different sources might enter data about a real-world object at different points in time. Thus, data about an object might differ. For instance, the address of a person can change, temperatures vary, prices fluctuate, etc. Again, these differences lead to different representations of the same real-world object and must be accounted by similarity measures.

Heterogeneous schemata. In general, different data sources use different schemata to represent same real-world entities. Schemata can be aligned using schema mapping technology. For instance, the attributes phone and fon have the same semantics and can be mapped to a common attribute in the integrated result. However, not all sources cover all attributes. For instance, one source may store the weight of a product, while the other source may not. Such missing attributes are padded with NULL values in the integrated result. Thus, even when sources agree on all common attributes, they are not necessarily exact duplicates.

Padding with NULL values ($\perp$) may lead to subsumed or complemented records. Table 1.2 shows three records from three different sources. Records r_1 and r_2 subsume r_3, and r_1 is complemented by r_2.

Table 1.2: Records r_1 and r_2 subsume r_3, and r_1 is complemented by r_2.				
r_1	John	Doe	(407) 356 8888	$\perp$
r_2	John	Doe	$\perp$	(407) 358 7777
r_3	John	Doe	$\perp$	$\perp$

Detecting such duplicates does not require a similarity measure and is thus easier than the general case with contradicting values. We do not cover the efficient detection of subsumed or complemented records but instead refer the reader to articles by Bleiholder et al. [2010], by Galindo-Legaria [1994], and by Rao et al. [2004].

1.3 USE CASES FOR DUPLICATE DETECTION

Duplicate detection comes in many guises and for many different applications. Apart from the term "duplicate detection", which we use throughout this lecture, the broad problem of detecting multiple representations of the same real-world objects has been named doubles, mixed and split citation problem, record linkage, fuzzy/approximate match, object/instance/reference/entity matching, object identification, deduplication, object consolidation, entity resolution, entity clustering, identity uncertainty, reference reconciliation, hardening soft databases, merge/purge, household matching, householding, and many more. Each mention might have a slightly different application or problem definition in mind, but each need two basic components – a similarity measure and an algorithm to explore the data.

   We now discuss several typical use cases for duplicate detection, each with a slightly different problem angle. The classical use case is that of customer relationship management, where duplicates within a large set of customer data are sought. Detecting duplicates in scientific databases emphasizes cleansing of data that is distributed and heterogeneous. Finally, the linked-open-data use case emphasizes more the unstructured and dynamic nature of data on the Web.

1.3.1 CUSTOMER RELATIONSHIP MANAGEMENT

Large organizations provide many points of contact with their customers: They might have an online store or information site, they might have walk-in stores, they might provide a phone hotline, they might have personal sales representatives, they might correspond via mail, etc. Typically, each point of contact is served by a separate data store. Thus, information about a particular customer might be stored in many different places inside the organization. In addition, each individual data set might already contain duplicates.

Figuratively speaking, when organizations communicate with a customer, the left hand does not know what the right hand is doing. Thus, revenue potential might be lost and customers might be dissatisfied; it is likely that most readers have experienced having to state the same information many times over. Managers have recognized the need to centrally integrate all information about a customer in so-called customer relationship management (CRM) systems. Apart from efficiently providing up-to-date customer information to the various applications of an organization, CRM systems must recognize and eliminate duplicates.

The domain of persons and companies is probably the most developed with respect to duplicate detection. Many specialized similarity measures have been devised specifically with that domain in mind. For instance, a duplicate detection system might encode a high similarity between the two dates-of-birth 5/25/71 and 1/1/71 even though they differ significantly: January 1st is a typical default value if only the year-of-birth of a customer is known. Other person-specific examples include accentuation-based similarity measures for last names, nickname-based similarity measures for first names, and specialized similarity measures for streets and zip codes.

1.3.2   SCIENTIFIC DATABASES

Scientific experiments and observations produce vast amounts of data. Prominent examples are the results of the human genome project or images produced by astronomical observation. Many such data sources are publicly available and thus very good candidates for integration. Many projects have arisen with the primary goal of integrating scientific databases of a certain universe of discourse, such as biological databases [Stein, 2003]. All such projects must solve the task of duplicate detection. If real-world objects or phenomena are observed and documented multiple times, possibly with different attributes, it is useful to recognize this and interlink or combine these representations. For instance, many proteins have been studied numerous times under different conditions. Combining and aggregating such data might avoid costly experiments [Hao et al., 2005; Trißl et al., 2005].

To this end, researchers have developed specialized similarity measures to cope with the fact that genomic data has two directly conflicting properties: (i) As it is generated in high-throughput experiments producing millions of data points in a single run, the data often have a high level of noise. (ii) Even slight variations in genomic sequences may be important to tell a real duplicate from a wrong one (think of the same gene in different yet closely related species).

Due to the vast amounts of data, scientific databases are usually not integrated into a large warehouse, but they are annotated with links to other representations in other databases [Karp, 1996]. Thus, the task of a researcher exploring a specific object is eased. In fact, large efforts have been invested to develop systems that allow integrated queries across these multiple sources [Bleiholder et al., 2004; Shironoshita et al., 2008].

1.3.3   DATA SPACES AND LINKED OPEN DATA

Duplicate detection is also relevant in scenarios beyond typical, well-formed data. We illustrate two use cases from domains with more heterogenous data. The first use case is the prime example for data spaces [Halevy et al., 2006], namely *personal information management* [Dittrich et al., 2009; Dong and Halevy, 2005]. Dataspaces comprise complex, diverse, interrelated data sources and are a generalization of traditional databases. The second, related use case introduces *linked open data* as a new form of publishing data on the (semantic) web. For both use cases, we show why duplicate detection is a necessary but difficult task.

Personal information management (PIM) can be considered as the management of an integrated view of all our personal data that, for instance, reside on our desktop, our laptop, our PDA, our MP3 player, etc. In addition to the heterogeneity of devices storing data, PIM also has to deal with the heterogeneity of data themselves, as relevant data encompass emails, files, address books, calendar entries, and so on. Clearly, PIM data do not correspond to the uniformly structured data we consider throughout this lecture[2]. For instance, a person described in an address book and a person being tagged on a picture may be duplicates, but it is highly unlikely that they share any other attributes (assuming we can distinguish attributes) than their name. Clearly, in this type of application, we need to first identify what data describe what type of object, and what data are semantically equivalent before being able to perform any reasonable comparisons. In data integration, this preprocessing step to duplicate detection is known as schema matching. For structured data, various algorithms for schema matching have been proposed [Rahm and Bernstein, 2001].

In PIM, due to the high variability of applications and data these applications store about objects, candidates of the same type may not share a sufficient number of attributes to decide if they represent the same real-world object. An extreme example where no common attribute exists is shown in Figure 1.5: Figure 1.5(a) shows an email whereas Figure 1.5(b) depicts a calendar entry. The email is addressed to `naumann@hpi.uni-potsdam.de` and concerns the Synthesis Lecture (see subject). The calendar describes a meeting that also contains Synthesis Lecture in its title, and the location refers to Felix' office at HPI. Both the email and the calendar entry refer to the same person, i.e., Felix Naumann, but based on the email address and the first name alone, it is very difficult to come to this conclusion. As a matter of fact, we most definitely cannot detect the duplicate reference to Felix Naumann by simply comparing person candidates based on their descriptions, assuming these have been extracted from the available data.

Beyond personal information, more and more data are publicly available on the Web. However, it is difficult to query or integrate this data. The semantic web community introduces and advocates the concept of *linked open data (LOD)* [Bizer et al., 2009b]. By assigning a URI to each object, referencing these objects with links, using the HTTP protocol, and finally by providing data sets openly (usually as sets of RDF triples), the hope is to create a large web of data from many sources that can be queried and browsed easily and efficiently. Indeed, a rapidly growing number of sources, such

---

[2]Note that this is generally true for data in data integration scenarios. Here, we chose PIM as a representative because related challenges are particularly accentuated.

(a) Email   (b) Calendar entry

Figure 1.5: Personal Information Management (PIM) Data

as DBpedia [Bizer et al., 2009a] or Freebase[3], constitute a wealth of easily accessible information. As of May 2009, the W3C reports over 70 data sets consisting of over 4.7 billion RDF triples, which are interlinked by around 142 million RDF links[4]. In many cases, these links represent duplicate entries. For instance, the entry of the Bank of America in Freebase stores a link to the corresponding Wikipedia entry.

Linked open data are from many very different domains of public, commercial, and scientific interest. The data sets are provided by many, often overlapping sources, making duplicate detection more important than ever. Much of the linking is currently performed manually, but automated methods can help. Because much of the data are heterogeneously structured and have large textual parts, similarity measures must be adapted accordingly. In addition, the sheer volume of data makes it all the more important to use efficient algorithms to find duplicate candidates.

1.4 LECTURE OVERVIEW

The remainder of this lecture is organized as follows: Chapter 2 formally introduces the problem of duplicate detection and describes its complexity. The following two chapters address the two specific problems of duplicate detection: Chapter 3 describes similarity measures to decide if two candidates are in fact duplicates, and Chapter 4 describes algorithms that decide which candidates to even consider. Finally, Chapter 5 shows how to evaluate the success of duplicate detection and Chapter 6 concludes the lecture. While this lecture is intended to serve as an overview and primer for the field of duplicate detection, we refer interested readers to a recent and more comprehensive literature survey by Elmagarmid et al. [2007].

---

[3]http://freebase.com
[4]http://esw.w3.org/topic/SweoIG/TaskForces/CommunityProjects/LinkingOpenData

CHAPTER 2

Problem Definition

As we have seen in Chapter 1, duplicate detection is a problem of highly practical relevance, and there is a need for efficient and effective algorithms to tackle the problem. Before delving into the details of such algorithms in the subsequent chapters, we first formally define the problem. More specifically, we start the discussion by providing a definition of the duplicate detection task in Section 2.1. This definition focuses on duplicate detection in data stored in a single relation, a focus we maintain throughout this lecture. We then discuss the complexity of the problem in Section 2.2. Finally, in Section 2.3, we highlight issues and opportunities that exist when data exhibit more complex relationships than a single relation.

2.1 FORMAL DEFINITION

Before we define duplicate detection, we summarize important concepts of the relational model and introduce their notation.

Given a relation R, we denote the schema of the relation as $S_R = \langle a_1, a_2, \ldots, a_n \rangle$. Each a_i corresponds to an attribute. A record stored in a relation R assigns a value to each attribute. We use two alternative notations for a record r, depending on which notation is better suited in the context it is used in: The first notation implies the schema and simply lists values, i.e., $r = \langle v_1, v_2, \ldots, v_n \rangle$; The second notation explicitly lists attribute-value pairs, that is, $r = \langle (a_1, v_1), (a_2, v_2), \ldots, (a_n, v_n) \rangle$. We assume that all data we consider for duplicate detection conform to a given schema.

Example 2.1 Figure 2.1 represents a relational table named Movie. The schema of the Movie relation is $\langle MID, Title, Year, Review \rangle$. The Movie relation contains four records, one being $\langle m1, BigFish, 2003, 8.1/10 \rangle$.

To properly define duplicate detection, we first have to decide which object representations are subject to deduplication. For instance, do we search only for duplicates within movies? Or do we

MID	Title	Year	Review
m1	Big Fish	2003	8.1 / 10
m2	Public Enemies	2009	7.4 / 10
m3	Public Enemies	09	⊥
m4	Big Fisch	2003	7.5 / 10

Figure 2.1: Sample Movie relation

search within all movies that were inserted or updated since the last deduplication of the database? Or do we want to identify duplicates only to those movies that do not have a review score? To specify the set of records that is subject to duplicate detection, we can simply formulate a query that retrieves these records. In our relational scenario, a possible SQL query to identify all records that describe movies that appeared since 2009 is simply

```
SELECT *
FROM Movie
WHERE Year >= 2009
```

The result of such a query is a set of records that corresponds to the set of records that need to be deduplicated. We refer to this set of records as the set of *duplicate candidates*, or *candidates* for short. A candidate has a specific type T that corresponds to the type of object that it represents, for instance, a movie. We denote the set of all candidates of type T as $C^T = \{c_1.c_2, \ldots, c_n\}$.

The next aspect we have to consider is that not all information included in an object representation is relevant for duplicate detection. In the relational context, this means that not every attribute of a record is relevant. For instance, whereas movie titles are relevant for duplicate detection as they are very descriptive of movies, the attribute Review is less descriptive of a movie, and hence, it is not suited to distinguish duplicates to a movie from non-duplicates. This observation leads us to the general definition of an object description.

Given a candidate c, the object description of c, denoted as $OD(c)$, is a set of attribute-value pairs that are descriptive of candidate c. That is, $OD(c) = \langle (a_1, v_1), (a_2, v_2), \ldots, (a_m, v_m) \rangle$. For a given candidate type T, the set of descriptive attributes of any candidate of type T is the same, i.e., all corresponding object descriptions contain attribute-value pairs for attributes $\{a_1, a_2, \ldots, a_m\}$. As a consequence, object descriptions are usually defined on schema level, and we can retrieve object descriptions by specifying SQL queries that return the desired attributes. As a simple example, we can retrieve the object description of movie $m1$ using the SQL query

```
SELECT Title, Year
FROM Movie
WHERE MID = 'm1'
```

Note that in practice, retrieving candidates and their corresponding description are usually combined into a single query. In our example, the SQL query is the same as the query for object descriptions shown above, except that the WHERE-clause is removed.

Having defined the input to duplicate detection algorithms, let us now move to the definition of the output. The ultimate goal of duplicate detection is to partition the set of candidates based on information provided by their object descriptions. Each partition returned by a duplicate detection algorithm contains candidates that all represent the same real-world object. Hence, we say that a partition represents a real-world object as well. The second property of the resulting partitions is that no two distinct partitions represent the same real-world object. We denote the final result of duplicate detection of candidates in C^T as the partitioning P^T.

Example 2.2   Let us assume that our set of candidates includes all movies described in the Movie relation shown in Figure 2.1. That is, $C^{Movie} = \{m1, m2, m3, m4\}$. Assuming that the object description of a movie consists of Title and Year only, we, for instance, have $OD(m1) = \{(Title, BigFish), (Year, 2003)\}$. The ideal result of duplicate detection is to identify that both the movie *Big Fish* and the Movie *Public Enemies* are each represented twice in the Movie relation. That is, ideally, a duplicate detection algorithm outputs $P^{Movie} = \{\{m1, m4\}, \{m2, m3\}\}$.

In contrast to our example, where duplicate detection results in a perfect classification, performing duplicate detection in practice does not reach the gold standard. Indeed, the similarity measure may miss some duplicates because their similarity is not high enough. These missed duplicates are referred to as false negatives. On the other hand, candidates may also be classified as duplicates although they are not because, despite a careful choice of descriptions, they still are very similar. We call this type of classification error false positives. As we discuss in Section 5.1, duplicate detection algorithms are designed to reduce the occurrence of at least one of these error types. Depending on the application, minimizing false positives may be more, less, or equally important to minimizing false negatives, so the choice of a proper duplicate detection algorithm and configuration depends on this characteristic.

The above definition of duplicate detection does not specify any details on algorithm specifics. As we see in subsequent chapters, numerous algorithms exist for duplicate detection. These have varying characteristics, and hence their runtime may significantly differ. A specific type of algorithm widely used throughout the literature and industry are iterative duplicate detection algorithms.

Iterative duplicate detection algorithms are characterized by the fact that they first detect pairs of duplicates, and they then exploit the transitivity of the is-duplicate-of relationship to obtain the desired duplicate partitions. Remember that two candidates are duplicates if they represent the same real-world object. Clearly, if A is duplicate of B, and B is duplicate of C, it is true that A is a duplicate of C, too.

Duplicate pairs are identified using a similarity measure $sim(c, c')$ that takes two candidates as parameters and returns a similarity score. The higher the result returned by the similarity measure, the more similar candidates are. If the similarity is above a given threshold, indicating that candidates have exceeded a certain similarity threshold θ, the two candidates are classified as duplicates and therefore form a duplicate pair. Again, thinking in terms of SQL queries, we may view iterative duplicate detection as a special type of join that, instead of using equality as join predicate, uses a similarity measure:

```
SELECT C1.* ,C2.*
FROM Movie AS C1, Movie AS C2
WHERE sim(C1,C2) > θ
```

To obtain partitions, let us model the set of candidates and duplicate pairs as a graph: a node represents a candidate and an edge exists between two candidates if they have been classified as duplicates because their similarity is above the threshold θ. Then, considering that the relationship "is-duplicate-of" is transitive, determining the partitions amounts to identifying all connected components in the graph. However, this may lead to partitions where two candidates are not similar at all where, in fact, there are no duplicates of each other. This is due to the fact that the similarity measure usually does not satisfy the triangle inequality; that is, $sim(A, B) + sim(B, C)$ is not necessarily greater or equal to $sim(A, C)$. As a simple example, let us assume that $sim(hook, book) > \theta$ and $sim(book, bosk) > \theta$. This is reasonable because each string does not differ by more than one character from the other string. However, it is easy to see that $hook$ and $bosk$ differ by two characters, yielding a lower similarity. In Section 4.3, we describe strategies to split up connected components that connect too dissimilar candidates due to long chains of pairwise duplicates in the graph.

2.2   COMPLEXITY ANALYSIS

In this section, we give an intuition of the general complexity of the problem. The complexity analysis of specific algorithms is part of their description in Chapter 4. For this general intuition, we focus on the runtime complexity of iterative duplicate detection algorithms.

In the setting of iterative duplicate detection, we perform one similarity comparison for every possible pair of candidates. Assuming that the similarity measure is symmetric, i.e., $sim(c, c') = sim(c', c)$, this means we have to perform $\frac{n \times (n-1)}{2}$ pairwise comparisons. To illustrate this, consider Figure 2.2 that shows the space of duplicate candidates for a database of 20 records. Each field $c_{i,j}$ in the matrix represents a comparison of the two corresponding candidates r_i and r_j. The diagonal fields $c_{i,i}$ need not be compared, nor do the fields in the lower part $c_{i,j}, i > j$. Thus, there remain $\frac{20(20-1)}{2} = 190$ comparisons (as opposed to 400 comparisons for the complete matrix).

Each invocation of the similarity measure adds to the complexity. The exact complexity of similarity computation depends on the actual similarity measure that is used. However, due to the fact that it bases its computation on object descriptions and relationship descriptions, both of which generally have a far smaller cardinality than C^T, we can view similarity computation as a constant factor compared to the number of necessary pairwise comparisons. This yields a complexity of $O(n^2)$ for detecting duplicate pairs. The final step is to obtain partitions that represent duplicates. This amounts to determining the connected components of a graph whose nodes are all candidates and where an edge exists between c and c' if and only if c and c' have been classified as duplicates. The connected components of a graph can be determined by a simple breadth-first-search or depth-first-search in linear time. More specifically, the complexity of this phase is $O(n + d)$, where d is the number of detected duplicate pairs. It is guaranteed that $d \leq n^2$ so forming the duplicate partitions can be performed, in the worst case in $O(n^2)$ and in practice, in far less time. As a consequence, the total runtime complexity of iterative duplicate detection is $O(n^2)$ for a given candidate set C^T that contains candidates of type T.

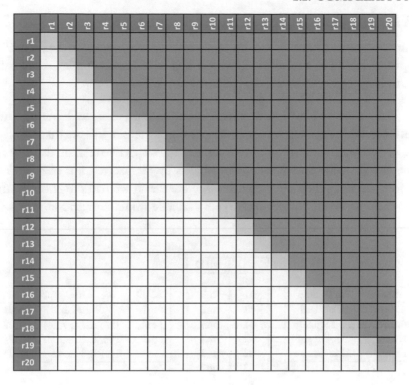

Figure 2.2: Matrix of duplicate candidates

Clearly, the quadratic time complexity described above is impractical for efficient duplicate detection on large databases. For instance, consider a small movie database with one million movie candidates. This would require approximately 5×10^{11} pairwise comparisons. Assuming a comparison can be done in 0.1 ms, the time for duplicate detection would roughly take one and a half years! Therefore, approaches to improve runtime have been devised. They all have in common that they aim at reducing the number of pairwise comparisons. We discuss these algorithms in more detail in Chapter 4. In practice, the number of comparisons performed can be reduced by up to 99%, compared to the number of comparisons necessary when using the naive, quadratic algorithm that compares all candidates with each other.

So far, we have discussed the theoretical runtime complexity that is dominated by the number of pairwise candidate comparisons. Another dimension to consider is the cost of disk accesses necessary to read the data from disk and to write the result back to disc. Each algorithm for duplicate detection devises its own strategy to minimize I/O cost. As we have seen, duplicate detection can be viewed as a special type of join. In the database literature, approaches to minimize I/O cost of joins is abundant, and we observe that duplicate detection algorithms use similar ideas to sort-merge-join or hash join.

2.3   DATA IN COMPLEX RELATIONSHIPS

Up to this point, we assumed that all data necessary for duplicate detection, i.e., candidates and their object descriptions, reside in a relation. However, data with more complex relationships exist: we may have multiple types of candidates that relate to each other.

Example 2.3   As an example for data in complex relationships, consider Figure 2.3, which extends Figure 2.1 with two additional relations, namely Actor and StarsIn. We see that two types of objects are described, i.e., actors and movies, and each tuple in the respective relation describes a single actor or movie. The StarsIn table does not describe objects by themselves, but rather relates objects to each other (more precisely, their representations). Note that if we had the entity relationship (ER) model for our example available, the object types available would correspond to the entities in the ER model.

AID	MID
a1	m1
a1	m2
a1	m3
a1	m4
a2	m2
a2	m3
a3	m1
a4	m4

AID	Firstname	Lastname
a1	Marion	Cotillard
a2	Johnny	Depp
a3	Ewen	McGregor
a4	Ewen	Mac Gregor

MID	Title	Year	Review
m1	Big Fish	2003	8.1 / 10
m2	Public Enemies	2009	7.4 / 10
m3	Public Enemies	09	$\perp$
m4	Big Fisch	2003	7.5 / 10

(a) Actor   (b) StarsIn   (c) Movie

Figure 2.3: Sample relations in a movie domain

In this setting, the general idea for duplicate detection is to exploit relationships between candidates in order to potentially increase the effectiveness of duplicate detection. That is, when comparing movie candidates, for instance, we can consider the actors starring in a movie in addition to a movie's object description (Title and Year). The PIM use case described in Section 1.3 is one scenario where duplicate detection benefits from relationships.

In Section 2.3.1, we extend the data model described in Section 2.1 to include multiple candidate types and their relationships. In Section 2.3.2, we then discuss challenges concerning similarity measurement that arise in this context, focusing on hierarchical and semi-structured XML data.

2.3.1   DATA MODEL

In this section, we extend the data model for the input and the output of duplicate detection to the case where we have more than one candidate type and where candidates relate to each other.

As we have seen, the input to duplicate detection when considering a single candidate type consists of a set of candidates and candidates are associated with object descriptions. This remains true for duplicate detection in data with complex relationships, however, we need to reflect the presence of multiple candidate types. Therefore, we define the candidate set $C = \{C^{T_1}, C^{T_2}, \ldots, C^{T_k}\}$ to contain sets of candidates, each of a different type. The definition of an object description is not affected; however, we point out that an object description needs to be defined for every candidate type.

Additionally, we need to model the relationships between candidates, so we can use them later during duplicate classification. In our example, the set of actors that play in a movie is very descriptive of a movie. Indeed, except for movie sequels, the casts of different movies usually differ significantly. To describe that other related candidates are relevant to detect duplicates to a candidate, we introduce the notion of relationship description. Intuitively, a relationship description of a given candidate contains all candidates that are descriptive of that particular candidate. More formally, given a candidate c of type T, its relationship description $RD(c) = \{c_1, c_2, \ldots, c_m\}$. Note that $c_i \in RD(c)$ does not necessarily have the same candidate type as $c_j \in RD(c)$, $i \neq j$, for instance, a movie may include both actors and awards in its relationship description.

Example 2.4   Considering movies and actors as candidates, we have $C^{Movie} = \{m1, m2, m3, m4\}$ and $C^{Actor} = \{a1, a2, a3, a4\}$, which we summarize in the candidate set $C = \{C^{Movie}, C^{Actor}\}$. The relationship description of a movie consists of the actors that star in that particular movie, for instance, $RD(m1) = \{a1, a3\}$.

Similar to object descriptions, relationship descriptions are usually defined on schema level using appropriate queries. These queries are usually based on domain-knowledge or they can be extracted from schema information, e.g., foreign keys. As an example, in order to retrieve the relationship description of $m1$, we may use the following query:

```
SELECT A.*
FROM Actor A, StarsIn S, Movie M
WHERE M.MID = 'm1' AND M.MID = S.MID AND S.MID = A.AID
```

Of course, to improve efficiency, the relationship descriptions of all candidates are retrieved using a single query, again by omitting the predicate M.MID = 'm1' that restricts the result to the relationship description of $m1$.

Concerning the output of duplicate detection in data with complex relationships, we trivially extend the output for a single candidate type to multiple candidates types, similar to our extension of the input candidate sets. More specifically, for every input candidate set C^{T_i}, we have an output partitioning P^{T_i}, which we summarize in the final output $P = \{P^{T_1}, P^{T_2}, \ldots, P^{T_k}\}$.

The way algorithms consider relationships to obtain the final partitioning may significantly differ from one algorithm to the other. For instance, different algorithms exist that specialize on duplicate detection of candidate types that relate to each other through different kinds of relationships (e.g., 1:N versus M:N), and their configuration allows to specify how relationships affect the duplicate detection process (see Section 4.2 for details).

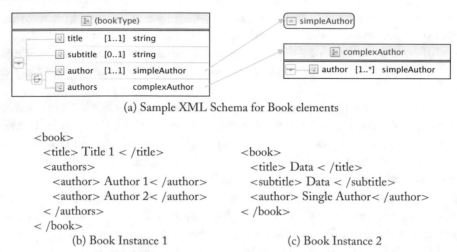

(a) Sample XML Schema for Book elements

```
<book>
  <title> Title 1 < /title>          <book>
  <authors>                            <title> Data < /title>
    <author> Author 1< /author>        <subtitle> Data < /subtitle>
    <author> Author 2< /author>        <author> Single Author< /author>
  < /authors>                        < /book>
< /book>
        (b) Book Instance 1                (c) Book Instance 2
```

Figure 2.4: Two XML instances complying to the same XML Schema

2.3.2   CHALLENGES OF DATA WITH COMPLEX RELATIONSHIPS

In this section, we describe challenges that arise when detecting duplicates in data with complex relationships. The general duplicate detection process that compares pairs of candidates still applies in this context, and the main challenges concern similarity measurement.

To represent data in complex relationships, we resort to an XML representation. XML allows semi-structured data and, using key and keyref constraints (similar to key and foreign key constraints in relational data), we can represent the general case where relationships between candidates form a graph. The fact that we use XML as data representation does not limit the generality of the discussion of challenges similarity measures have to face; we simply use XML to better convey the general ideas.

A basic assumption that still applies to duplicate detection algorithms for data with complex relationships is that the data comply to a predefined schema. However, even if data comply to the same schema, instances may not be equally structured. As an example, consider the XML Schema definition represented in Figure 2.4. The two XML elements shown in Figure 2.4 (b) and (c) both comply to the schema depicted in Figure 2.4(a). However, their structure differs in the following aspects that represent additional challenges for duplicate detection.

Element optionality. An element can be defined as optional in XML Schema, so an instance may or may not contain that element. This is, for instance, the case with the subtitle element that occurs either zero or one time as it needs only exist when the described book has a subtitle. In the relational case, the structure of data is given, and the only means of specifying that a value is not further specified is the use of a NULL value. This choice exists in XML in addition to element optionality.

Element context. An element may appear in various contexts within an XML hierarchy, or, in general, in a graph of relationships. The context of an XML element is given by its nesting in the XML hierarchy, for instance, identified by a path expression from the root element. The schema essentially specifies where an XML element can occur. As an example, the author element may be a child of book, in case the book has only one author. Otherwise, an author appears in a sequence of authors and has the path book/authors/author.

Element cardinality. In a relational schema, one attribute exists exactly once and has exactly one value. In XML, an element can exist from zero to infinitely many times. In our example, within a sequence of authors (complexAuthor type), the author element can exist from one to n times (denoted by *).

The three properties of XML data described above cause additional challenges for duplicate detection, compared to the purely relational case.

First, element optionality adds another dimension of unknown information to be treated by the duplicate detection algorithm, or, more specifically, by the similarity measure. The semantics of an element having a NULL value are not necessarily the same as the semantics of an element not existing at all. For instance, if book has a subtitle element, but the value is NULL, this may signify that we actually know that the book has a subtitle, but we do not know the exact value. In contrast, the fact that a subtitle element is missing (as in Figure 2.4(b)) may indicate that the book simply has no subtitle. In general, similarity measures need to devise a strategy to deal with the possibly different semantics of missing elements and NULL values. Clearly, in the relational case where the schema is given and rigid, there are no alternative ways of representing missing information.

Second, due to the fact that the same XML element type can appear in different contexts (for instance, author), we can no longer assume, even if the data comply to the same schema, that the structure of candidates aligns perfectly. To illustrate the problem, assume we consider both books and authors as candidates. In determining relationship descriptions, we have to search for all the different contexts authors may appear in. Otherwise, we may miss some related candidates. That is, the definition of candidates and their descriptions is more complex than in the relational case. Another issue to consider is again the semantics behind each context. When author is a direct child of book, the semantics may be that we know that there is exactly one author of that book. On the contrary, if we observe one author nested under the authors element, the author list may be longer, but the remaining authors are not known. For instance, assume we compute the similarity of two books whose descriptions are equal except for the single author allowed by the schema. We may decide that the similarity score in this case is lower than, for instance, the similarity of two books being equal except for one author in the sequence of authors both candidates have. Such a fine distinction is not necessary for data complying to a relational schema. As a consequence, when processing XML data, we need to be aware of this distinction and decide how to handle the subtle differences it may cause, notably during similarity computation.

The third property, the element cardinality adds complexity to similarity measurement when we consider duplicate detection in relational data with relationships between candidate types. Indeed, it is true that zero or more candidates of the same type may occur in the relationship description of a given candidate. When computing the similarity of two candidates based on their relationship description, different possibilities to align the candidates in the relationship descriptions exist. As an example, assume that a book has a further **annotation** element that includes tags that people added to a book. These annotations are part of a relationship description. Now, assume $RD(Book1) = \{goat, oat\}$ and $RD(book2) = \{boat, moat\}$[1]. Based on similarity between candidates within relationship descriptions, it is unclear whether *goat* matches *boat* or *moat* and whether *oat* matches *boat* or *moat*. Note that when considering object descriptions in relational data, candidates of the same type all have the same schema. In this case, each attribute occurs exactly once, so a 1:1 matching between the attribute-value pairs of two candidates is sufficient to compare their object descriptions. In XML, elements being part of the object description may occur zero or more times, so the more complex comparison that requires to identify a best match applies to object descriptions as well.

In this section, we discussed challenges in computing similarities between candidates in scenarios where data includes complex relationships. In Section 3.4, we discuss similarity measures that have explicitly been defined for XML that (partially) address the above issues and in Section 4.2.2, we describe algorithms that consider relationships.

---

[1]We slightly abuse notation here and use the unique object description value of an annotation to represent an annotation candidate within a relationship description

CHAPTER 3

Similarity Functions

In Chapter 2, we provided a formal definition of general duplicate detection and formalized a special case of duplicate detection, namely iterative duplicate detection. We have seen that iterative duplicate detection uses a similarity measure to classify a candidate pair as duplicate or non-duplicate. More specifically, given a similarity threshold θ, we classify two candidates c and c' using a similarity measure sim by

$$classify(c, c') = \begin{cases} c \text{ and } c' \text{ are duplicates} & \text{if } sim(c, c') > \theta \\ c \text{ and } c' \text{ are non-duplicates} & \text{otherwise} \end{cases}$$

In practice, more than two classes may be used, for instance, a third class for "possible duplicates" is often used.

In this chapter, we discuss various similarity measures that have been used for duplicate detection throughout the literature. In fact, we discuss both similarity measures and distance measures. When using a similarity measure $sim(\cdot)$, the intuition is that the higher the similarity of two candidates, the more likely it is that they are duplicates. A distance measure, which we denote as $dist(\cdot)$ measures exactly the opposite of similarity: The larger the distance between two candidates, the less likely it is that they are duplicates. Clearly, when using a distance measure, thresholded classification of duplicates needs to be adapted. Formally,

$$classify(c, c') = \begin{cases} c \text{ and } c' \text{ are duplicates} & \text{if } dist(c, c') \leq \theta \\ c \text{ and } c' \text{ are non-duplicates} & \text{otherwise} \end{cases}$$

In the case of normalized similarity measures that return a similarity between zero and one, a corresponding distance score can be computed as $dist(c, c') = 1 - sim(c, c')$.

In our discussion, we distinguish different classes of measures. In Section 3.1, we discuss token-based measures that take as input a pair of sets of tokens. Edit-based measures, covered in Section 3.2, on the other hand, take as input a pair of strings. Token-based and edit-based measures can be combined into hybrid measures, which we discuss in Section 3.3. All these measures only consider object descriptions, and in Section 3.4, we describe several similarity measures that exploit information from relationship descriptions as well. The discussion on similarity measures ends in Section 3.5 with a brief description of further similarity measures. We then discuss another technique, orthogonal to similarity measures, to classify pairs of candidates as duplicates or non-duplicates. The essence of the technique is to define domain-specific rules (see Section 3.6).

3.1   TOKEN-BASED SIMILARITY

Token-based similarity measures compare two strings by first dividing them into a set of tokens using a tokenization function, which we denote as $tokenize(\cdot)$. Intuitively, tokens correspond to substrings of the original string. As a simple example, assume the tokenization function splits a string into tokens based on whitespace characters. Then, the string *Sean Connery* results in the set of tokens $\{Sean, Connery\}$. As we will show throughout our discussion, the main advantage of token-based similarity measures is that the similarity is less sensitive to word swaps compared to similarity measures that consider a string as a whole (notably edit-based measures). That is, the comparison of *Sean Connery* and *Connery Sean* will yield a maximum similarity score because both strings contain the exact same tokens. On the other hand, typographical errors within tokens are penalized, for instance, the similarity of *Sean Connery* and *Shawn Conery* will be zero.

We discuss three token-based measures in this section: The basic Jaccard coefficient can be used to compute the similarity as discussed in Section 3.1.1. We then present a more sophisticated similarity measure that introduces weights of tokens in Section 3.1.2. In defining these two measures, we assume that tokens do not overlap, that is, each character of the original string exists in exactly one token. In Section 3.1.3, we discuss how q-grams, which are considered overlapping tokens, are used for similarity measurement. The main advantage of using overlapping tokens is that the similarity is affected less by typographical errors than when using non-overlapping tokens.

3.1.1   JACCARD COEFFICIENT

The Jaccard coefficient is a similarity measure that, in its most general form, compares two sets P and Q with the following formula:

$$Jaccard(P, Q) = \frac{|P \cap Q|}{|P \cup Q|} \tag{3.1}$$

Essentially, the Jaccard coefficient measures the fraction of the data that is shared between P and Q, compared to all data available in the union of these two sets.

In the context of duplicate detection, the question is what are the sets P and Q? Throughout the duplicate detection literature, we observe two basic uses of the Jaccard coefficient: tokens are either obtained from strings [Monge and Elkan, 1996], or they correspond to complete descriptions [Bilenko et al., 2003]. The first variant is useful to identify similar pairs of descriptions in hybrid similarity measures (see Section 3.3) whereas the second variant computes the similarity of candidates.

String comparison based on the Jaccard coefficient. Given a tokenization function $tokenize(s)$ that tokenizes a string s into a set of string tokens $\{s_1, s_2, \ldots, s_n\}$, we compute the Jaccard coefficient of two strings s_1 and s_2 as

$$StringJaccard(s_1, s_2) = \frac{|tokenize(s_1) \cap tokenize(s_2)|}{|tokenize(s_1) \cup tokenize(s_2)|} \tag{3.2}$$

Candidate comparison based on the Jaccard coefficient. Given two candidates, we have seen in Section 2.1 that these are compared based on their respective object description. The Jaccard coefficient of two candidates c_1 and c_2 is given by

$$DescriptionJaccard(c, c') = \frac{|OD(c_1) \cap OD(c_2)|}{|OD(c_1) \cup OD(c_2)|} \qquad (3.3)$$

Example 3.1   Consider a scenario where Person is a candidate type. One way to represent the name of a person in a database is to store the complete name in one attribute, e.g., the Name attribute. Hence, Person candidates have a description attribute Name. Now, consider two candidates where the Name descriptions have values *Thomas Sean Connery* and *Sir Sean Connery*, respectively. Assuming a tokenization function that separates a string into tokens based on whitespace, we obtain

$$\begin{aligned} tokenize(\textit{Thomas Sean Connery}) &= \{\textit{Thomas, Sean, Connery}\} \\ tokenize(\textit{Sir Sean Connery}) &= \{\textit{Sir, Sean, Connery}\} \end{aligned}$$

We observe that among these two token sets, there are only four distinct tokens, and both *Sean* and *Connery* appear in both sets. Consequently, applying the Jaccard coefficient to these two strings results in

$$StringJaccard(\textit{Thomas Sean Connery, Sir Sean Connery}) = \frac{2}{4}$$

To illustrate candidate comparison based on the Jaccard coefficient, let us now assume that a person's name is split into several attributes in the Person relation, i.e., title, first name, middle name, and last name. Keeping the same example, we now have

$$\begin{aligned} OD(c_1) &= \{(firstname, Thomas), (middlename, Sean), (lastname, Connery)\} \\ OD(c_2) &= \{(title, Sir), (middlename, Sean), (lastname, Connery)\} \end{aligned}$$

In these two sets, we observe that the middlename and the lastname description are equal in $OD(c_1)$ and $OD(c_2)$ and in total, we have four distinct descriptions. As a result, again

$$DescriptionJaccard(c_1, c_2) = \frac{2}{4}$$

Based on this simple example, we point out several deficiencies of the Jaccard similarity. First, we observe that the fact that one name is simply missing a title value penalizes the similarity significantly. Intuitively, such a title (or the lack thereof) should have less impact on similarity than the last name or first name, for instance. In the next section, we discuss the cosine similarity measure that addresses this issue. A second drawback of Jaccard similarity is that it is very sensitive to typographical errors in single tokens. For instance, *Shean Conery* and *Sean Connery* have a similarity of zero. In Section 3.1.3, we show how token-based similarity measures can be adapted to penalize typographical errors less. As a final remark, note that if *Sean* would have been put in the firstname attribute (which is likely to be the case, e.g., when a Web-form requires a first name but no middle name), *DescriptionJaccard* would yield a result of $\frac{1}{5}$, unless we specify that middlename and firstname shall be considered equal. None of the similarity measures described in this chapter can explicitly cope with this problem, and it is often assumed that such information is used when initializing descriptions in order to avoid the problem.

An advantage of the Jaccard coefficient is that it is not sensitive to word swaps. Indeed, the score of two names *John Smith* and *Smith John* would correspond to the score of exactly equal strings because the Jaccard coefficient considers only whether a token exists in a string, not at which position.

3.1.2   COSINE SIMILARITY USING TOKEN FREQUENCY AND INVERSE DOCUMENT FREQUENCY

The cosine similarity is a similarity measure often used in information retrieval. In general, given two n-dimensional vectors V and W, the cosine similarity computes the cosine of the angle α between these two vectors as

$$CosineSimilarity(V, W) = \cos(\alpha) = \frac{V \cdot W}{||V|| \cdot ||W||} \tag{3.4}$$

where $||V||$ is the length of the vector $V = [a, b, c, \ldots]$ computed as $\sqrt{a^2 + b^2 + c^2 + \ldots}$. In duplicate detection, the vectors V and W can represent either tokens in a string or descriptions of a candidate. Note that we made the same distinction in the discussion of the Jaccard coefficient. From now on, we illustrate only the case where tokens arise from tokenizing string values, but readers should keep in mind that this is not the only possible use of the token-based measures we discuss.

Assuming we tokenize two strings s_1 and s_2 using a tokenization function $tokenize(\cdot)$, the question arises how we build the two vectors V and W from the tokens. We discuss the solution in two steps: first, we discuss the dimensionality d of these two vectors before we focus on what numbers are filled in these vectors.

Essentially, the d dimensions of these vectors correspond to all d distinct tokens that appear in any string in a given finite domain, denoted as $\mathcal{D}$. In our scenario, we assume that s_1 and s_2 originate from the same relational attribute, say a. In this case, $\mathcal{D}$ corresponds to all distinct tokens in all values of a. For large databases, this number of tokens may be large, so the vectors V and W have high dimensionality d in practice.

At this point of the discussion, we know how large the vectors V and W are. Let us now discuss what data these vectors contain. For this, we first consider the term vector $\mathcal{T}$ of $\mathcal{D}$, which, of course, is d-dimensional as well. This term vector contains a weight for each of the d distinct tokens in $\mathcal{D}$. This weight reflects how relevant a token is in $\mathcal{D}$, relative to other tokens. To weigh tokens, the token frequency-inverse document frequency (*tf-idf*) is commonly used both in information retrieval and duplicate detection. To define the *tf-idf* score, we first need to define its individual components, namely *tf* and *idf*.

Essentially, the term frequency measures how often a token occurs in a given string value. Intuitively, the term frequency reflects the relevance of a token within a string value: the more often a token occurs, the more relevant it is in the context of the string value. As an example, consider a Web-page about the International Space Station ISS. The token *ISS* is likely to appear frequently on this web page, definitely more frequently than on a web-page about the Airbus 380. This results in a high term frequency of *ISS* on the ISS Web-page and a low term frequency of *ISS* on the Airbus Web-page. Assuming that a token t appears in the value v of an object description of a candidate c such that $(a, v) \in OD(c)$, we denote its term frequency as $tf_{t,c}$.

The intuition behind the inverse document frequency is that it assigns higher weights to tokens that occur less frequently in the scope of all candidate descriptions. This is useful as it assigns low weights to common tokens in a domain, e.g., in a database listing insurance companies, the token *Insurance* is likely to occur very frequently across object descriptions and the *idf* thus assigns it a lower weight than to more distinguishing tokens such as *Liberty* or *Prudential*. Formally, we compute the inverse document frequency of a token t occurring in the object description of a candidate c as

$$idf_{t,c} = \frac{n}{|\{c|(a, v) \in OD(c)\} \wedge t \in tokenize(v)|} \tag{3.5}$$

The *tf-idf* score combines both the term frequency and the inverse document frequency into a single score, using the following formula:

$$tf\text{-}idf_{t,c} = \log\left(tf_{t,c} + 1\right) \times \log\left(idf_{t,c}\right) \tag{3.6}$$

As a reminder, n is the total number of candidates.

We compute the *tf-idf* score for every token $t_i \in \mathcal{D}$ and set the i-th value in the term vector $\mathcal{T}$ to this score. Finally, to create vectors V and W, we simply set the i-th value in V and W to the i-th weight in $\mathcal{T}$ if the strings that V and W represent actually contain the i-th token, and to zero otherwise. We can now compute the cosine similarity as described by Equation 3.4.

Example 3.2   Figure 3.1 shows ten US insurance companies, which we consider as candidates whose type we denote as $T = IC$. We provide candidate identifiers in Figure 3.1 for future reference. These are not part of an insurance company's description that consists only of the company name. We observe that any token occurs at most once in a value of attribute Name, so the token frequency $tf_{Insurance,c_i}$ is either 0 or 1 for a given candidate c_i. We further observe that among the ten candidates, six contain the token *Insurance* so $idf_{Insurance,c_i} = \frac{10}{6}$. Based on these values, we obtain, for instance, $tf\text{-}idf_{Insurance,c_4} = \log(1 + 1) \times \log\left(\frac{10}{6}\right) \approx 0.07$. Similarly, we obtain $tf\text{-}idf_{Farmers,c_4} \approx 0.30$ and $tf\text{-}idf_{Liberty,c_7} = 0.30$.

We now can compute the cosine similarity between the two strings $s_1 = $ *Farmers Insurance* and $s_2 = $ *Liberty Insurance*. Based on the tokens that s_1 and s_2 contain, we obtain the following vectors V and W as depicted in Figure 3.2, assuming the order of strings in $\mathcal{Q}$ shown.

CID	Name
c_1	Allstate
c_2	American Automobile Association
c_3	American National Insurance Company
c_4	Farmers Insurance
c_5	GEICO
c_6	John Hancock Insurance
c_7	Liberty Insurance
c_8	Mutual of America Life Insurance
c_9	Safeway Insurance Group
c_{10}	Westfield

Figure 3.1: Sample table listing insurance companies

Q	V	W
Allstate	0	0
America	0	0
Automobile	0	0
Association	0	0
National	0	0
Insurance	0.07	0.07
Company	0	0
Farmers	0.30	0
GEICO	0	0
John	0	0
Hancock	0	0
Liberty	0	0.30
...	0	0

Figure 3.2: Example on computing the cosine similarity between *Farmers Insurance* and *Liberty Insurance*

Using Equation 3.6, we finally obtain $CosineSimilarity(V, W) = \dfrac{0.07^2}{\sqrt{0.07^2 + 0.30^2}} \approx 0.05$. We observe that the similarity score is extremely low, although, at first sight, the strings overlap in half their tokens. However, the token they overlap in is *Insurance*, which has a very low weight because it appears in a large fraction of the candidates. As a consequence, the similarity score is low, too. Note that in this example, the Jaccard similarity yields a similarity of 0.33.

From the example above, we see that the cosine similarity better reflects the distinguishing power of tokens, compared to the Jaccard similarity due to different weights assigned to tokens. These weights can be computed using *tf-idf*, but we could use any other weight function as well, for instance, a function specifically designed for a particular domain. Note that it is also possible to use the weight function in combination with other similarity measure than the cosine similarity.

We further point out that it is often the case that, like in our example, attribute values used as descriptions contain a token at most once, yielding sparse vectors when using *tf-idf* as weight function. However, it is easy to see that the vectors can easily be compressed to include only the positions where at least one of the two vectors has a non-zero value, which actually corresponds to a vector containing only tokens of *tokenize*(s_1) $\cup$ *tokenize*(s_2).

Besides the advantage that the relevance of tokens is better reflected using cosine similarity with *tf-idf* weights, the cosine similarity is also not sensitive to word swaps. A drawback of the cosine similarity as described in this section is the fact that it cannot cope with typographical errors. Two means to overcome this problem are the use of q-grams, discussed next, and the definition of the *softTFIDF*, which we discuss in Section 3.3.3.

3.1.3   SIMILARITY BASED ON TOKENIZATION USING q-GRAMS

In q-gram based similarity measures, tokens are not determined based on special characters such as whitespace or punctuation. Instead, a string is divided into smaller tokens of size q. These tokens are referred to as q-grams or n-grams. Another difference to tokens we discussed previously is that these tokens overlap, i.e., one character in a string appears in several tokens (actually, exactly q tokens). To generate q-grams of size q, we slide a window of size q over the string to be tokenized and each sequence of characters within the window is a token. To obtain q tokens with the first and last characters of a string, we introduce a special character not in the initial alphabet and pad the string with this character.

Example 3.3   Generating q-grams.   Consider strings $s_1 = $ *Henri Waternoose* and $s_2 = $ *Henry Waternose*. We generate 3-grams (also called trigrams) for the two strings that result in the sets of 3-grams below. Note that we use underscore (_) to represent a whitespace and the padding characters at the beginning and the end of a string are denoted as #.

$$q\text{-grams of } s_1 \quad = \quad \{\text{##H, #He, Hen, enr, nri, ri\_, i\_W, \_Wa, Wat, ate, ter, ern, rno, noo, oos, ose, se#, e##}\}$$
$$q\text{-grams of } s_2 \quad = \quad \{\text{##H, #He, Hen, cnr, nry, ry\_, y\_W, \_Wa, Wat, ate, ter, ern, rno, nos, ose, se#, e##}\}$$

Given two sets of q-grams, it is possible to consider these tokens to compute the token-based similarity measures described in Sections 3.1.1 and 3.1.2, which, as the following example illustrates results in a similarity score that is less sensitive to typographical errors than the previously described measures.

Example 3.4 q-gram based token similarity computation.   Let us reuse the two strings s_1 and s_2 and their corresponding sets of q-grams described in Example 3.3. We observe that the two token sets overlap in 13 q-grams, and we have a total of 22 distinct q-grams. Using the Jaccard similarity (see Section 3.1.1), we obtain *StringJaccard*$(s_1, s_2) = \frac{13}{22} = 0.59$. Using the cosine similarity with *tf-idf* weights, we obtain

$$CosineSimilarity(V, W) = \frac{1.04^2 \times 13}{\sqrt{1.04^2 \times 13 + 1.34^2 \times 5} \times \sqrt{1.04^2 \times 13 + 1.34^2 \times 4}} \approx 0.64$$

where V and W are the q-gram sets of s_1 and s_2, respectively.

3.2   EDIT-BASED SIMILARITY

Let us now focus on a second family of similarity measures, so called edit-based similarity measures. In contrast to token-based measures, strings are considered as a whole and are not divided into sets of tokens. However, to account for errors, such as typographical errors, word swaps and so on, edit-based similarities allow different *edit operations* to transform one string into the other, e.g., insertion of characters, character swaps, deletion of characters, or replacement of characters.

3.2.1   EDIT DISTANCE MEASURES

In general, the edit distance between two strings s_1 and s_2 is the minimum cost of transforming s_1 into s_2 using a specified set of edit operations with associated cost functions. The cost of the transformation than simply is the sum of the costs of the individual edit operations. In this section, we limit the discussion to a simple variant of the edit distance that is known as the Levenshtein distance and we show how to compute it using a dynamic programming algorithm. Readers interested in more details on the subject are invited to read the overview article on approximate string matching by Navarro [2001].

Given two strings s_1 and s_2, the Levenshtein distance $LevDist(s_1, s_2)$ is equal to the minimum number of character insertions, deletions, and replacements necessary to transform s_1 into s_2.

Example 3.5   Levenshtein distance.   As an example, consider the two strings $s_1 = Sean$ and $s_2 = Shawn$. The Levenshtein distance of these two strings is 2, as we need to (i) replace the e in s_1 by an h and (ii) insert a w to s_1 to transform s_1 into s_2. Obviously, there are infinitely many possibilities to transform s_1 into s_2, e.g., we may delete all characters of s_1 and subsequently insert all characters of s_2. However, the number of edit operations in this case would be 9, which is not minimal.

A popular algorithm to compute the Levenshtein distance is based on dynamic programming. It starts by initializing a $(|s_1| + 1) \times (|s_2| + 1)$ matrix $\mathcal{M}$, where $|s|$ denotes the length of a string s. Once initialized, we fill the matrix $\mathcal{M}$ with values computed using the equations below. We denote the value in the i-th column and j-th row of $\mathcal{M}$ as $\mathcal{M}_{i,j}$, with $0 \leq i \leq |s_1|$ and $0 \leq j \leq |s_2|$. The i-th character in a string s_1 is denoted as $s_{1,i}$.

$$\mathcal{M}_{i,0} = i \tag{3.7}$$
$$\mathcal{M}_{0,j} = j \tag{3.8}$$
$$\mathcal{M}_{i,j} = \begin{cases} \mathcal{M}_{i-1,j-1} & \text{if } s_{1,i} = s_{2,j} \\ 1 + min\left(\mathcal{M}_{i-1,j}, \mathcal{M}_{i,j-1}, \mathcal{M}_{i-1,j-1}\right) & \text{otherwise} \end{cases} \tag{3.9}$$

Computation proceeds from the top left of the matrix to the bottom right. Once all values in the matrix have been computed, the result of the algorithm that corresponds to the Levenshtein distance can be retrieved from $\mathcal{M}_{|s_1|,|s_2|}$.

Example 3.6   Computing the Levenshtein distance using dynamic programming.   Consider again the two strings $s_1 = Sean$ and $s_2 = Shawn$. Figure 3.3(a) shows the matrix $\mathcal{M}$ after we

		S	h	a	w	n
	0	1	2	3	4	5
S	1					
e	2					
a	3					
n	4					

		S	h	a	w	n
	0	1	2	3	4	5
S	1	0	1	2	3	4
e	2					
a	3					
n	4					

		S	h	a	w	n
	0	1	2	3	4	5
S	1	0	1	2	3	4
e	2	1	1	2	3	4
a	3	2	2	1	2	3
n	4	3	3	2	2	**2**

(a) State after initializing first row and first column

(b) State after applying Equation 3.9 to second row

(c) Final state with edit distance stored in bottom right corner

Figure 3.3: Computing the edit distance using a dynamic programming approach

initialized the matrix and computed the values of the first row and first column. Let us now focus on Figure 3.3(b), which shows the state of the algorithm after processing the second row in the matrix. At $M_{1,1}$ we see that the first characters of s_1 and s_2 match, so we look at position $M_{0,0}$ to determine the value we should fill in (first line of Equation 3.9). All remaining fields in this row are filled using the second line of Equation 3.9 because none of the other characters in s_2 match the first character, i.e., S of s_1. It is worth pointing out that the first line of Equation 3.9 essentially represents a diagonal lookup of a value, whereas the second line looks up and left of the current position, determines the minimum of all three fields, and adds one to this minimum cost. The final result of the algorithm corresponds to Figure 3.3(c)[1]. According to this matrix, *LevDist*(Sean, Shawn) = 2.

As mentioned at the beginning of this section, the Levenshtein distance is a special case of an edit distance as it uses unit weight and three basic edit operators (insert, delete, and replace character). Although widely used in practice for duplicate detection, the Levenshtein distance is not a suitable similarity measure when whole segments of a string differ, e.g., when one string is a prefix of the second string (*Prof. John Doe* vs. *John Doe*) or when strings use abbreviations (*Peter J Miller* vs. *Peter John Miller*). These problems are primarily due to the fact that all edit operations have equal weight and that each character is considered individually. Further edit distance measures have been proposed to cope with these problems, including the Smith-Waterman distance and the use of affine gaps. We do not discuss these measures in detail (they all use concepts and algorithms similar to those used to compute the Levenshtein distance) but highlight their effect on the final distance score.

Intuitively, the Smith-Waterman distance allows to identify the longest common subexpression between two strings [Smith and Waterman, 2001]. For instance, it determines that the longest common subexpression between $s_1 = $ *Prof. John Doe* and $s_2 = $ *John Doe* is the string *John Doe*. Based on this output of the Smith-Waterman distance, we can now argue that this common subexpression actually corresponds to s_2, which is simply missing a prefix compared to s_1. Conceptually, we divide the strings into a prefix, a common subexpression, and a suffix and can assign lower weights to the

---

[1]It is possible to determine the actual operations to transform s_1 into s_2 with minimum cost; however, this is not pertinent to duplicate detection, and we thus omit the discussion.

insertion or deletion of blocks of size l (a block corresponds to a prefix or suffix) than to the insertion of l individual characters. Hence, using the Smith-Waterman distance, the existence of a prefix or a suffix is less penalized than in the Levenshtein distance.

The Smith-Waterman distance divides the original strings into a prefix, a common subexpression, and a suffix. This, however, is not sufficient to lower the penalty of gaps *within* the string, e.g., due to abbreviations, missing words, etc. Essentially, it does not reflect the case where several common subexpressions, divided by non-matching character sequences exist. This problem is addressed by the affine gap distance [Waterman et al., 1976]: It allows edit operations, notably insertion and deletion of complete blocks within a string and assigns these block insertions and deletions less weight than to the insertion or deletion of the individual characters in a block. As an example, let $s_1 = $ *Peter J Miller* and $s_2 = $ *Peter John Miller*. We see two common subexpressions, i.e., *Peter J* and *_Miller*, and one block of characters that needs to be inserted in order to transform s_1 into s_2, i.e., *ohn*. The cost of this block can be computed as the cost of opening a block o plus the cost e of extending the block by one character. Hence, the cost of inserting this block is, for instance, $o + 2e = 1 + 2 \times 0.1 = 1.2$, given $o = 1$ and $e = 0.1$. This cost is lower than the cost of inserting three characters in the Levenshtein distance (the cost would be 3 using unit weights for character insertion). Consequently, the affine gap distance gives the possibility to penalize less the non-matching blocks of characters within a string, which is beneficial when comparing strings that contain abbreviations or that are missing some tokens.

3.2.2   JARO AND JARO-WINKLER DISTANCE

In this section, we discuss two similarity measures that account for mismatches in two strings by allowing character transpositions, an edit operation we have not seen so far. Also, their computation is not based on dynamic programming.

The Jaro similarity [Jaro, 1989] essentially compares two strings s_1 and s_2 by first identifying characters "common" to both strings. Two characters are said to be common to s_1 and s_2 if they are equal and if their positions within the two strings, denoted as i and j, respectively, do not differ by more than half of the length of the shorter string. Formally, $|i - j| \leq 0.5 \times min(|s_1|, |s_2|)$. Once all common characters have been identified, both s_1 and s_2 are traversed sequentially, and we determine the number t of transpositions of common characters where a transposition occurs when the i-th common character of s_1 is not equal to the i-th common character of s_2. Given the set σ of common characters and the number of transpositions t, the Jaro similarity is computed as

$$JaroSim = \frac{1}{3} \times \left(\frac{|\sigma|}{|s_1|} + \frac{|\sigma|}{|s_2|} + \frac{|\sigma| - 0.5t}{|\sigma|} \right)$$

Example 3.7   Let $s_1 = $ *Prof. John Doe* and $s_2 = $ *Dr. John Doe*. Thus, $|s_1| = 14$ and $|s_2| = 12$. The maximum distance between two common characters then is $0.5 \times min(12, 14) = 6$. The set of common characters is $\sigma = \{r, ., \_, J, o, h, n, \_, D, o, e\}$, where $\_$ denotes a space character. We

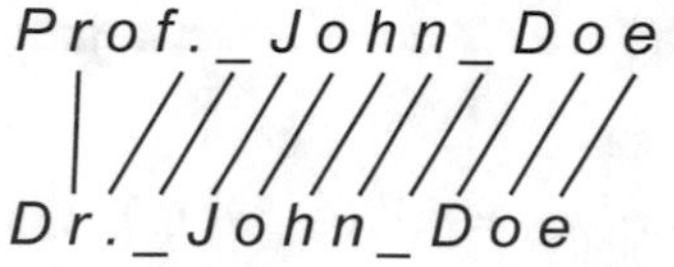

```
Prof._John_Doe
|/////////
Dr._John_Doe
```

Figure 3.4: Matching characters between *Prof. John Doe* and *Dr. John Doe* used by the Jaro distance

illustrate the common characters in Figure 3.4. We see that none of the matching lines crosses another matching line, which indicates that none of the common characters yields to a transposition, so we have $t = 0$. The final Jaro distance thus is

$$JaroSim(s_1, s_2) = \frac{1}{3} \times \left(\frac{11}{12} + \frac{11}{14} + \frac{11-0}{11} \right) \approx 0.9$$

The Jaro similarity generally performs well for strings with slight spelling variations. However, due to the restriction that common characters have to occur in a certain distance from each other, the Jaro distance does not cope well with longer strings separating common characters. As a simple example, consider s_1 = *Professor John Doe* and s_2 = *John Doe*. We can identify only two common characters, as illustrated in Figure 3.5. This yields a low similarity score of 0.45 although s_1 is the same as s_2 except for a (long) prefix. The same exercise can be repeated for the case where one string is equal to the other except for an additional suffix.

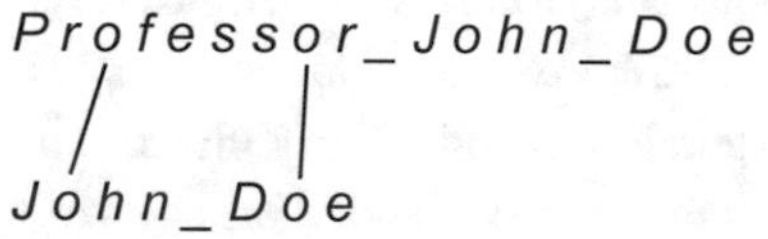

```
Professor_John_Doe
          /    |
       John_Doe
```

Figure 3.5: Matching characters between *Professor John Doe* and *John Doe* used by the Jaro distance

In the domain of person names, which is a widely studied domain with highly specialized measures, it is true that the problem described above mostly occurs for names with a common prefix but where one name has an additional suffix (e.g., *Peter J* vs. *Peter John* stored as a first name). An extension of the Jaro similarity, called the Jaro-Winkler similarity [Winkler and Thiboudeau, 1991], considers this special case. Given two strings s_1 and s_2 with a common prefix ρ, the Jaro-Winkler similarity is computed as

$$JaroWinklerSim(s_1, s_2) = JaroSim(s_1, s_2) + |\rho| \times f \times (1 - JaroSim(s_1, s_2))$$

where f is a constant scaling factor for how much the similarity is corrected upwards based on the common prefix ρ.

Example 3.8 Let s_1 = *Peter* and s_2 = *Peter Jonathan*. These two strings have 5 common characters that correspond to the common prefix ρ = *Peter*. Clearly, there are no permutations of characters in σ so $t = 0$. It follows that $JaroSim(s_1, s_2) = 0.78$. Assuming a scaling factor $f = 0.1$ the Jaro-Winkler similarity is equal to

$$JaroWinklerSim(s_1, s_2) = 0.78 + 5 \times 0.1 \times (1 - 0.78) = 0.89$$

3.3   HYBRID FUNCTIONS

In Section 3.1, we discussed token-based similarity measures that divide the data used for comparisons into sets of tokens, which are then compared based on equal tokens. We further discussed similarity measures that keep data as a whole in the form of a string and that compute the similarity of strings based on string edit operations that account for differences in the compared strings.

In this section, we discuss similarity measures that combine both tokenization and string similarity in computing a final similarity score. We refer to these algorithms as hybrid similarity functions. The measure covered in Section 3.3.1 extends Jaccard similarity to also include similar tokens in the set of overlapping descriptive data. The second hybrid measure, discussed in Section 3.3.2, is the Monge-Elkan measure. Finally, Section 3.3.3 covers an extension of the cosine similarity using $tf\text{-}idf$ for weight computation.

3.3.1   EXTENDED JACCARD SIMILARITY

We first describe two extensions to the Jaccard similarity that have been proposed throughout the literature [Ananthakrishna et al., 2002; Weis and Naumann, 2005]. The first extension accounts for similar tokens and the second extension introduces weight functions.

Let s_1 and s_2 be two strings that can be divided into sets of tokens by a tokenization function, denoted as $tokenize(\cdot)$. In the original definition of the Jaccard similarity (see Section 3.1.1), only equal tokens are part of the intersection of the token sets of s_1 and s_2. The idea behind the first extension of the Jaccard similarity is to also include similar tokens in the intersection to allow for small errors, e.g., typographical errors between shared tokens.

Formally, let $TokenSim(t_1, t_2)$ be a string similarity measure that compares two tokens $t_1 \in tokenize(s_1)$ and $t_2 \in tokenize(s_2)$. Any of the string similarity measures discussed in Section 3.2 can be applied here. We define the set of shared similar tokens between s_1 and s_2 as

$$Shared(s_1, s_2) \quad = \quad \{(t_i, t_j)|t_i \in tokenize(s_1) \wedge t_j \in tokenize(s_2) : TokenSim(t_i, t_j) > \theta_{string}\}$$

where θ_{string} is a secondary similarity threshold. Similarly, we define the tokens unique to s_1 as

$$Unique(s_1) = \{t_i|t_i \in tokenize(s_1) \wedge (t_i, t_j) \notin Shared(s_1, s_2)\}$$

Analogously, the tokens unique to s_2 are defined by

$$Unique(s_2) = \{t_j|t_j \in tokenize(s_2) \wedge (t_i, t_j) \notin Shared(s_1, s_2)\}$$

A second extension of the Jaccard similarity that is commonly used in combination with the previous one is to introduce a weight function w for matching and non-matching tokens. For instance, token pairs in *Shared* may get a weight that corresponds to their similarity. An aggregation function $\mathcal{A}$ then aggregates the individual weight.

Using the two extensions above, the hybrid Jaccard similarity is defined as

$$HybridJaccard = \frac{\mathcal{A}_{(t_i,t_j)\in Shared(s_1,s_2)}\,w(t_i,t_j)}{\mathcal{A}_{(t_i,t_j)\in Shared(s_1,s_2)}\,w(t_i,t_j) + \mathcal{A}_{(t_i)\in Unique(s_1)}\,w(t_i) + \mathcal{A}_{(t_j)\in Unique(s_2)}\,w(t_j)}$$

Note that instead of a secondary string similarity measure, we may also use a string distance measure to identify similar tokens. In this case, we simply replace $TokenSim(t_i,t_j) > \theta_{string}$ by $TokenDist(t_i,t_j) \leq \theta_{string}$. As a final remark, it is also possible to use different weight functions for $Shared(s_1,s_2)$, $Unique(s_1)$, and $Unique(s_2)$. For instance, if token similarity is used as weight function for $Shared(s_1,s_2)$, we have to use another function for both $Unique$ sets, because we simply have no similarity scores within these sets.

Example 3.9 Hybrid Jaccard similarity Let $s_1 = $ *Henri Waternoose* and $s_2 = $ *Henry Peter Waternose*. Using any of the token-based similarity measures we discussed, the similarity is zero assuming tokenization based on whitespaces. Indeed, the two strings do not share any equal token. Using the hybrid Jaccard similarity measure, we obtain

$$Shared(s_1,s_2) = \{(Henri, Henry), (Waternoose, Waternose)\}$$

when using the Levenshtein distance and $\theta_{string} = 1$ to determine similar tokens. It follows that $Unique(s_1) = \emptyset$ and $Unique(s_2) = \{Peter\}$. Let us further assume that we use unit weights for $Unique$ sets, whereas the weight of similar tokens (t_i,t_j) is given by $1 - \frac{LevDist(t_i,t_j)}{max(|t_i|,|t_j|)}$. The aggregation function $\mathcal{A}$ simply sums up individual weights. Based on these assumptions, the result of the hybrid Jaccard similarity is

$$HybridJaccard(s_1, s_2) = \frac{0.8 + 0.9}{0.8 + 0.9 + 0 + 1} = 0.63$$

3.3.2 MONGE-ELKAN MEASURE

Let us now discuss the Monge-Elkan similarity measure [Monge and Elkan, 1996]. Intuitively, it first tokenizes two strings s_1 and s_2 and matches every token t_i from s_1 to the token t_j in s_2 that has the maximum similarity to t_i, i.e., where $TokenSim(t_i,t_j)$ is maximal. These maximum similarity scores obtained for every token of s_1 are then summed up, and the sum is normalized by the number of tokens in s_1. Formally, the Monge-Elkan distance is defined by

$$MongeElkanSim(s_1, s_2) = \frac{1}{|tokenize(s_1)|} \sum_{i=1}^{|tokenize(s_1)|} \max_{j=1}^{|tokenize(s_2)|} TokenSim(t_i, t_j)$$

Example 3.10   Let us compare two strings $s_1 = $ *Henri Waternoose* and $s_2 = $ *Henry Peter Waternose*. The token of s_2 with maximum similarity to *Henri* is obviously *Henry*, and the most similar string to *Waternoose* is *Waternose*. Let us assume that the two maximum similarity scores equal 0.8 and 0.9, respectively. Then, we obtain

$$MongeElkanSim(s_1, s_2) = \frac{0.8 + 0.9}{2} = 0.85$$

3.3.3   SOFT TF/IDF

The final hybrid similarity measure we discuss extends the cosine similarity based on *tf-idf* in the same spirit as the extension of Jaccard: similar strings, as determined by a secondary string similarity measure further increase the similarity. Again, let $TokenSim(t_1, t_2)$ be a secondary string similarity function used to compare tokens. Let $Close(\theta_{string}, s_1, s_2)$ be the set of tokens $t_i \in tokenize(s_1)$ such that there is some $t_j \in tokenize(s_2)$ where $TokenSim(t_i, t_j) > \theta_{string}$. That is,

$$Close(\theta_{string}, s_1, s_2) = \{t_i | t_i \in tokenize(s_1) \wedge \exists t_j \in tokenize(s_2) : TokenSim(t_i, t_j) > \theta_{string}\}$$

Note that opposed to the definition of $Shared(s_1, s_2)$ that we use to compute extended Jaccard similarity, $Close(\theta_{string}, s_1, s_2)$ only includes tokens from string s_1 and not from s_2. Tokens from s_2 similar to tokens from s_1 included in *Close* are considered using the following equation that determines the most similar token $t_j \in tokenize(s_2)$ to any $t_i \in Close(\theta_{string}, s_1, s_2)$:

$$maxsim(t_i, t_j) = \max_{t_j \in tokenize(s_2)} TokenSim(t_i, t_j)$$

Then, the hybrid version of the cosine similarity measure, called *softTFIDF* is defined as

$$SoftTFIDF(s_1, s_2) = \sum_{t_i \in Close(\theta_{sim}, s_1, s_2)} \left(\frac{\textit{tf-idf}_{t_i}}{||V||} \times \frac{\textit{tf-idf}_{t_j}}{||W||} \times maxSim(t_i, t_j) \right)$$

where V and W are the vector representations of s_1 and s_2 containing *tf-idf* scores described in Section 3.1.2.

Example 3.11 Soft TF/IDF.   Let us illustrate *softTFIDF* reusing the strings $s_1 = $ *Henri Waternoose* and $s_2 = $ *Henry Peter Waternose*. As an example, assume that the vector representations of these two strings, respectively, are

$$V = \{0.6, 0.6, 0, 0, 0\}$$
$$W = \{0, 0, 0.5, 0.3, 0.6\}$$

We determine $Close(\theta_{string}, s_1, s_2) = \{Henri, Waternoose\}$ because for both of these tokens, a similar token exists in s_2. Then, the hybrid cosine similarity is

$$softTFIDF(s_1, s_2) = \frac{0.6}{\sqrt{0.6^2 + 0.6^2}} \times \frac{0.5}{\sqrt{0.5^2 + 0.3^2 + 0.6^2}} \times 0.8$$
$$+ \frac{0.6}{\sqrt{0.6^2 + 0.6^2}} \times \frac{0.6}{\sqrt{0.5^2 + 0.3^2 + 0.6^2}} \times 0.9$$
$$\approx 0.79$$

The main difference between the Monge-Elkan similarity and *softTFIDF* is that the Monge-Elkan similarity assumes all tokens to have equal weight whereas *softTFIDF* uses *tf-idf* scores to reflect the distinguishing power of a token in a token weight. Another, more subtle difference is that the *SoftTFIDF* only considers similarities between tokens that are above a given threshold θ. Such a threshold is not present in the Monge-Elkan similarity where any token in s_1 is matched to a token in s_2, no matter how low the similarity between these two tokens may be.

To summarize, all hybrid measures combine the benefits of both token-based and edit-based measures for duplicate classification: edit-based measures account for errors within tokens whereas token-based measures account for errors related to missing tokens and token swaps.

3.4   MEASURES FOR DATA WITH COMPLEX RELATIONSHIPS

All measures discussed so far consider only the object description of candidates. As we have seen in Section 2.3, it is possible to further consider relationships between candidates. In this section, we provide an overview of similarity measures devised specifically for duplicate detection in semi-structured data, most notably, for XML data. More similarity measures that consider relationship descriptions of candidates exist, but these usually are extensions of token-based similarity measures that consider related candidates similarly to tokens [Weis, 2008].

The discussion of Section 2.3.2 shows that challenges for similarity measures arise when dealing with semi-structured XML data. As a reminder, these challenges arise due to element optionality, element context, and varying element cardinality. Throughout the literature, three similarity measures have explicitly been defined for XML.

The structure-aware XML distance measure [Milano et al., 2006] computes the distance between two XML elements based on their substructure, that is, the substructure stands in as a description of the candidate that corresponds to the root XML element. To compare two candidates, an overlay between their two subtrees is computed. Informally, an overlay computes a weighted 1:1 matching between the two subtrees, so that nodes or leaves are matched only if they have the same path from the root. That is, it is not possible to match the same XML elements in different contexts. The weight assigned to a match is based on a distance measure, e.g., edit distance for string values in leaves. Several possible overlays may exist, and the goal is to determine an overlay with minimal cost (sum of match weights) and such that the overlay is not a proper substructure of any other possible overlay. Once such an overlay has been determined, the distance between the two candidates is simply the cost of the overlay. We observe that the different semantics of both element optionality and element context are not distinguished, but element cardinality is not a problem.

The approach presented by Leitão et al. [2007] constructs a Bayesian network, taking two XML elements as input, each rooted in the candidate element and having a subtree that corresponds to the description. Nodes in the Bayesian network represent duplicate probabilities of (i) a set of simple XML elements, (ii) a set of complex XML elements, (iii) a pair of complex elements, or (iv) a pair of simple elements[2]. The algorithm that constructs the Bayesian network assumes that each XML element occurs in exactly one context. Probabilities are propagated from the leaves of the Bayesian network (that correspond to probabilities of pairs of simple elements) to the root and can be interpreted as similarities. As nodes either represent pairs or sets of elements, the different semantics of a missing element vs. a NULL value cannot be captured because the lack of an element results in the probability node not being created at all.

The DogmatiX similarity measure [Weis and Naumann, 2005] is aware of the three challenges described in Section 2.3.2 that arise when devising a similarity measure for XML data. However, DogmatiX does not distinguish between the different semantics that both element optionality and element context allow. On the other hand, DogmatiX distinguishes between XML element types and real-world types so that all candidates of the same type are treated as such, even though they may occur in a different context. Essentially, to compute the DogmatiX similarity, we form pairs of descriptions (there is no distinction between object description and relationship description) and divide them into two sets: similar description pairs and singleton descriptions. A similar description pair is defined as a pair of descriptions whose pairwise string similarity, for instance, computed based on the string edit distance, is above a given threshold. Any description that is not part of any similar description pair is a singleton description. The set of singleton descriptions is further pruned to account for the fact that some descriptions cannot have a similar partner due to different cardinalities of elements of that type. Both similar and singleton descriptions are weighted based on a variation of the inverse document frequency. The overall similarity is the ratio of the sum of weights of all similar description pairs over the sum of weights of all descriptions (similar or singleton).

In summary, we observe that all similarity measures proposed for XML duplicate detection cope with varying element cardinality, whereas only DogmatiX explicitly considers the problem

---

[2]A simple XML element is an XML element that nests only a text node. Complex XML elements, on the other hand, nest only XML elements and no text node.

of element context when generating descriptions. None of the similarity measures distinguishes between possibly different semantics caused by alternative representations of missing data or by different element contexts when computing a similarity score. It remains an open research issue to define measures that make these distinctions and to investigate how these distinctions affect the quality of duplicate detection. Besides specialized similarity measures for XML, we also point out algorithms that improve efficiency by pruning comparisons by exploiting properties of hierarchically structured data in Section 4.2.1.

3.5   OTHER SIMILARITY MEASURES

The measures discussed so far are the most widely used for duplicate detection. However, none of these measures are applicable to all conceivable scenarios. As we have seen, some of the measures specialize on short strings with few typographical errors whereas others have been devised to be insensitive to word swaps. In this section, we summarize similarity measures for three further special cases, i.e., phonetic similarity, numeric similarity, and structural similarity.

Phonetic similarity. Whereas previously discussed measures focus on string similarity, phonetic similarity focuses on the sounds of spoken words, which may be very similar despite large spelling differences. For instance, the two strings *Czech* and *cheque* are not very similar; however, they are barely distinguishable phonetically. Therefore, they have a large phonetic similarity.

Soundex is a very common phonetic coding scheme, and the idea behind the computation of phonetic similarity is to first transform strings (or tokens) into their phonetic representation and to then apply the similarity measures on strings or tokens on the soundex representation [Bourne and Ford, 1961].

Numeric similarity. None of the discussed measures are of much use when comparing numerical data. Typically, numbers are simply considered as strings, which yields unsatisfactory results, for instance, when comparing *1999* and *2000*. A solution is to measure the difference of two numbers compared, e.g., by computing $|1999 - 2000|$. However, in different domains, the difference in numbers has different meanings. For instance, when measuring differences on a microscopic scale, a difference of 1 mm is a large difference, whereas on a macroscopic scale 1 mm is almost nothing. A possible way to "normalize" such a difference is to take the distribution of values in the domain into account.

Structural similarity. As a final remark, we point out that none of the similarity measures discussed so far considers the structure of the data; they all focus on content. However, considering the structure may also be relevant, e.g., when comparing trees that correspond to XML data. The most widely known structural similarity measure is the *tree edit distance* and variations thereof [Shasha et al., 1994]. Essentially, the tree edit distance is an edit-based distance measure (such as the Levenshtein distance), but instead of allowing edit operations on characters of a string, it considers edit operations on nodes of a tree structure. Due to its high computational complexity, it is rarely used for duplicate detection.

3.6   RULE-BASED RECORD COMPARISON

Up to this point, we have discussed similarity measures and distance measures that compute a real-valued score. This score is then input to a duplicate classifier as described at the beginning of this chapter (see p. 23). As a reminder, if the similarity score, as returned by a similarity measure, is above a given threshold θ, the compared pair of candidates is classified as a duplicate and as a non-duplicate, otherwise.

In this section, we discuss a complementary method to similarity measures for classifying candidate pairs as duplicates or non-duplicates: Rule-based record comparison approaches build rules on attributes (or combinations of attributes) to make a classification. These rules may use similarity measures for attribute comparisons. An example of such a rule for two **Person** candidates c_1 and c_2 is:

$$
\begin{aligned}
& \textit{first name of } c_1 \textit{ is similar to first name of } c_2 \\
\wedge \quad & \textit{last name of } c_1 \textit{ equals last name of } c_2 \\
\Rightarrow \quad & c_1 \textit{ and } c_2 \textit{ are duplicates}
\end{aligned}
$$

We note that in contrast to similarity measures that apply to any string data from any domain, rule-based approaches make use of domain knowledge and are thus domain-specific approaches to duplicate classification. We discuss two variants of rule-based record comparisons, namely an approach that builds on equational theory [Hernández and Stolfo, 1998], and profile-based comparisons [Doan et al., 2003; Weis et al., 2008].

3.6.1   EQUATIONAL THEORY

In this section, we describe an approach that compares two candidates c_1 and c_2 using implications of the form

$$ P \Rightarrow c_1 \equiv c_2 $$

where P is a complex predicate over attributes in the candidates' object descriptions, i.e., in $OD(c_1) \cup OD(c_2)$, and the equivalence relationship between c_1 and c_2 signifies that these candidates are considered duplicates. A set of such rules composes a domain-specific equational theory that allows to classify candidates based on a set of rules.

Let us consider the predicate P more closely: P is a boolean expression that can be written in conjunctive normal form, i.e., as a conjunction of (disjunctions of) terms:

$$ P = (term_{1,1} \vee term_{1,2}, \vee \ldots) \wedge (term_{2,1} \vee term_{2,2} \vee \ldots) \wedge \ldots \wedge (term_{n,1} \vee term_{n,2} \vee \ldots) $$

Zooming in on the actual terms, the equational theory allows virtually any comparison between attribute values. However, to make sensible comparisons, these comparisons apply to common attributes of c_1 and c_2. Indeed, it would not make much sense to use gender information for comparison if only c_1 (and not c_2) contained gender information. We introduce an example that clarifies the concept of an equational theory.

Example 3.12 Equational theory.   Consider a person database PersDB1 that contains the records depicted in Figure 3.6(a) and a second person database PersDB2 represented in Figure 3.6(b). We observe that not all information is represented in both databases. Indeed, whereas name and social security number (ssn) are represented in both sources (albeit using different representations in the case of person names), age is present only in PersDB1 and salary is stored only in PersDB2.

ssn	fname	mname	lname	age
123	Peter	John	Miller	46
345	Jane		Smith	33
678	John	Jack	Doe	9

(a) PersDB1

ssn	name	salary
123	Peter Miller	80k
345	Jane B. Smith	60k
679	Jack John Doe	100k

(b) PersDB2

Figure 3.6: Two sample Person databases

To identify duplicate persons among PersDB1 and PersDB2, suppose we use the following three rules to compare two candidate persons c_1 and c_2:

$$c_1.ssn = c_2.ssn \wedge concat(c_1.fname, c_1.mname, c_1.lname) \approx c_2.name \Rightarrow c_1 \equiv c_2$$
$$c_1.ssn = c_2.ssn \wedge substr(c_1.lname, c_2.name) \wedge substr(c_1.fname, c_2.name) \Rightarrow c_1 \equiv c_2$$
$$substr(c_1.fname, c_2.name) \wedge substr(c_1.mname, c_2.name) \wedge substr(c_1.lname, c_2.name) \Rightarrow c_1 \equiv c_2$$

We observe that terms may use complex comparison functions: for instance, in the first rule, we first concatenate the three name components of c_1 and then compare the concatenated result to the name of c_2, using similarity ($\approx$) as comparison operator. This operator indicates that the two strings being compared need to be similar, which is, for instance, determined using one of the previously defined similarity measures. In the remaining two rules, $substr(l, r)$ denotes that the string l is a substring of r.

Let us now compare all persons in PersDB1 with all persons in PersDB2. We observe that when comparing both records with $ssn = 123$, Rule 1 is not satisfied because PersDB2 is missing the middle name. However, the second rule identifies these two representations to be duplicates because the social security numbers are equal and the first name and the last name in PersDB1 occur in the corresponding name field in PersDB2. Finally, Rule 3 fails to identify the duplicate again, because PersDB2 does not contain the middle name of *Peter Miller*. Applying these rules, we find two more duplicates: Rule 2 classifies both tuples with ssn = *345* as duplicates and Rule 3 determines the tuples with ssn = *678* and ssn = *679* to be duplicates.

3.6.2   DUPLICATE PROFILES

In the equational theory discussed in Section 3.6.1 rules are used exclusively to classify duplicates. If none of the rules qualifies two candidates as duplicates, they are implicitly classified as non-duplicates. Let us refer to the rules of equational theory as positive rules. In addition to these rules, it is possible to add so called negative rules to the equational theory [Weis et al., 2008]. These classify pairs of candidates as non-duplicates and have the form:

$$P \Rightarrow c_1 \not\equiv c_2$$

where P is again a complex predicate as described in Section 3.6.1.

Example 3.13   Negative rule.   Reusing the sample tables of Figure 3.6, a possible negative rule is

$$c_1.ssn \neq c_2.ssn \Rightarrow c_1 \not\equiv c_2$$

This rule excludes candidates c_1 and c_2 being duplicates if their social security numbers do not match.

We can combine positive and negative rules as a sequence of classifiers to form a duplicate profile, such that pairs not classified by classifier i are input to the subsequent classifier $i + 1$. It is interesting to note that the order of rules in a profile that mixes positive and negative rules affects the final output, in contrast to equational theory where the output is always the same no matter the order of the rules. As a simple example, assume we had applied the negative rule of Example 3.13 before Rule 3 of Example 3.12. Then, the pair of Persons with respective ssn of *678* and *679* would be classified as non-duplicates and they would not be passed on to the classifier using Rule 3, so they are not classified as duplicates.

Both positive rules and negative rules only use information that is present in both candidates. In the case where both c_1 and c_2 contribute additional, non-shared information, it is possible to further refine a duplicate profile based on this information [Doan et al., 2003]. Intuitively, the idea is to make a plausibility check of a duplicate classification to possibly revoke a previous classification based on the combined information of c_1 and c_2. This plausibility check can be done using hard constraints similar to the negative rules that revoke a preliminary duplicate classification. A second possibility is to further use soft constraints that do not decide by themselves, but rather output their confidence in a pair being a duplicate. The individual confidence scores are finally combined to yield a final classification result.

CHAPTER 4

Duplicate Detection Algorithms

As presented in Chapter 2, the problem of duplicate detection needs two components for its solution. After reviewing similarity measures to decide upon duplicity of candidate pairs we now turn to the second component – algorithms that decide which candidates to compare.

With Figures 2.2 we had motivated the quadratic search space as a matrix of candidate pairs. The goal of the algorithms presented in Section 4.1 is to reduce the number of comparisons while not compromising the quality of the result. If not all candidates are compared, there is the danger of missing some duplicates. Chapter 5 elaborates on this tradeoff. In Section 4.2, we discuss algorithms that are suited for data with complex relationships. Those algorithms have in common that they detect pairs of duplicates and form duplicate partitions by simply computing the transitive closure based on pairwise classification results. In Section 4.3, we discuss more sophisticated clustering algorithms to obtain duplicate partitions.

4.1 PAIRWISE COMPARISON ALGORITHMS

To avoid a prohibitively expensive comparison of all pairs of records, a common technique is to carefully partition the records into smaller subsets. If we can assume that duplicate records appear only within the same partition, it is sufficient to compare all record-pairs within each partition. Two competing approaches are often cited: Blocking methods strictly partition records into disjoint subsets, for instance, using zip codes as partitioning key. Windowing methods, in particular the Sorted-Neighborhood method, sort the data according to some key, such as zip code, and then slide a window of fixed size across the sorted data and compare pairs only within the window. Both methods can be enhanced by running multiple partitioning/windowing passes over the data.

4.1.1 BLOCKING

Blocking methods pursue the simple idea of partitioning the set of records into disjoint partitions (blocks) and then comparing all pairs of records only within each block [Ananthakrishna et al., 2002; Baxter et al., 2003; Bilenko et al., 2006]. Thus, the overall number of comparisons is greatly reduced. Given n records and b partitions, the average size of each partition is $\frac{n}{b}$. In each partition each record pair must be compared, which yields a total number of pairwise comparisons of

$$b \cdot \frac{\frac{n}{b}(\frac{n}{b} - 1)}{2} = \frac{n(\frac{n}{b} - 1)}{2} = \frac{1}{2}\left(\frac{n^2}{b} - n\right)$$

assuming all partitions are of equal size. Table 4.1 (see page 48) gives an overview of the computational complexity of the different methods compared to the exhaustive approach of comparing all pairs of records.

Figure 4.1 repeats the matrix from Figure 2.2 (p. 17). Assume that records 1 – 20 are sorted by the partitioning key, both horizontally and vertically. The candidate pairs after partitioning are shaded. Clearly, there are much fewer candidates than before, namely only 47 compared to the complete matrix with 190 pairs.

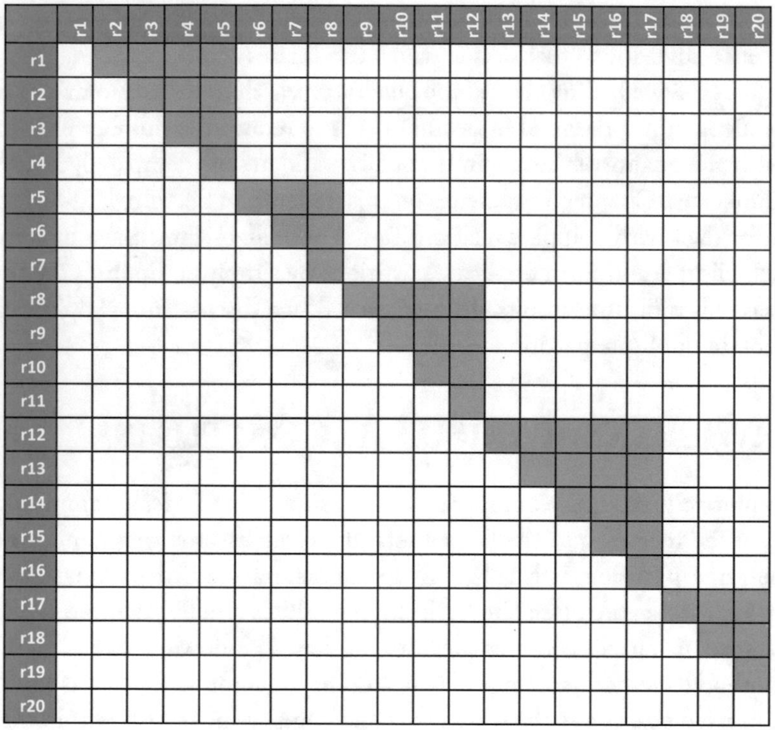

Figure 4.1: Matrix of duplicate candidates with blocking algorithm.

An important decision for the blocking method is the choice of a good partitioning predicate, which determines the number and size of the partitions. They should be chosen in a manner that potential duplicates appear in the same partition. For example, for CRM applications a typical partitioning is by zip code or by the first few digits of zip codes. The underlying assumption is that duplicates have the same zip code, i.e., there is no typo in the zip code and the customer has not moved from one zip code to another. If two duplicate records have the same zip code, they appear in the same partition and thus can be recognized as duplicates. Other partitionings might be by last name or some fixed-sized prefix of them, by street name, by employer, etc. In general, partitions of roughly the same and predictable size are preferable. For instance, partitioning by the first letter of the last name yields several very small partitions (q, x, ...) and some very large partitions (m, s, ...). Especially comparing all pairs in these large partitions can make the problem infeasible.

To drop the assumption that duplicates have the same partitioning key, a *multi-pass method* can be employed. That is, the blocking algorithm is run multiple times, each time with a different partitioning key. The chance that a duplicate pair does not appear together in at least one of the partitions is very low. It would have to contain errors in every attribute that is used for partitioning.

After the multiple runs, the transitive closure is formed over all detected duplicates because duplicity is inherently a transitive relation, and thus more correct duplicate pairs can be reported. Even within a single run, the transitive closure returns duplicates that were missed by the similarity measure: With an edit distance threshold of 1, *Maine St.* is close to *Main St.*, which, in turn, is close to *Moin St.*. Thus, even though all three strings might appear within the same block, only two pairs are recognized as duplicates, and the third pair is discovered only through transitivity.

4.1.2   SORTED-NEIGHBORHOOD

Windowing methods, such as the Sorted-Neighborhood method, are slightly more elaborate than blocking methods. Hernández and Stolfo [1995, 1998] describe the Sorted-Neighborhood Method (SNM), which is divided into three phases. In the first phase, a sorting key is assigned to each record. The key does not have to be unique and can be generated by concatenating characters (or substrings of values) from different attributes. It is useful to carefully select values based on the probability of errors. For instance, it is more likely to err in a vowel than in a consonant, and it is less likely to err in the first letter of a name. Thus, a key for a customer record could be defined as:

first 3 constants of last name | first letter of last name | first 2 digits of zip code

In the second phase, all records are sorted according to that key. As in the blocking method, the assumption is that duplicates have similar keys and are thus close to each other after sorting. The first two phases are comparable to the selection of a partitioning predicate and the actual partitioning in the blocking method.

The final, third phase of SNM slides a window of fixed size w across the sorted list of records. All pairs of records that appear in the same window are compared. Thus, when sliding the window, one record moves out of the window and a new record enters it. Only this new record must be compared with the remaining $w - 1$ records. The size of the window represents the trade-off between efficiency and effectiveness; larger windows yield longer runtimes but detect more duplicates. In experiments, window sizes between 10 and 30 have been reported to be effective. Figure 4.2 shows the candidate pair matrix with those pairs shaded that are compared by SNM with a windows size of 4. Again, the number of comparisons is reduced from 190 to 54.

The sorting key should be chosen distinct enough so that the number of records with the same key is not greater than the window size. Otherwise, not all records with the same key are compared and duplicates may be overlooked. A more distinct key enable a more fine-tuned sorting. Also, the first few characters of the key are obviously more important than the last few. Thus, one should choose attributes that are likely to contain few errors for the first characters of the sorting key.

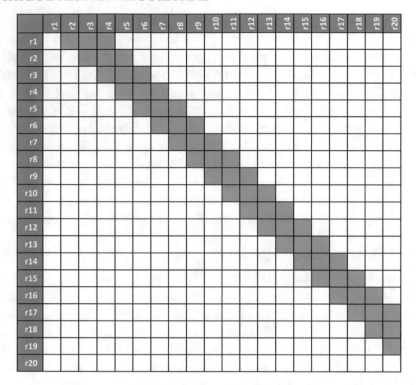

Figure 4.2: Matrix of duplicate candidates with the Sorted-Neighborhood algorithm.

As opposed to the blocking method, SNM requires a transitive closure step not only due to the nature of the similarity measure but also because duplicates appear in different partitions/windows: Figure 4.3 shows a situation where two duplicate pairs are found within different windows and only the transitive closure produces the complete set of duplicate pairs. Records r3, r3', and r3" are all duplicates, but r3 and r3" never appear within the same window of size 4. Only the transitive closure using their mutual duplicity with r3' reveals that they too are duplicates.

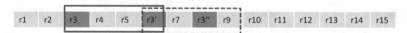

Figure 4.3: Transitive closure for SNM even after a single pass.

As for the blocking method, there is a chance that the sorting characters contain errors. To avoid mis-sorts, multi-pass variants of SNM produce multiple keys and perform the sorting and windowing multiple times. As with the blocking method, the transitive closure is finally calculated. The Multipass Sorted-Neighborhood method is summarized here:

1. Choose set of keys K.

2. For each key $k \in K$:

   (a) Sort records according to k.

   (b) Slide window over records comparing all pairs within a window.

3. Determine transitive closure

The implementation of SNM is usually done with the help of a DBMS: Using a surrogate key for the records, key creation generates a temporary table with the surrogate key column along with one column for each sorting key. In each pass, this temporary table, is sorted by the corresponding sorting key column and joined with the main table to fetch the records to be compared. Thus, it can be expected that each run needs only three read-passes over the data – one to create the keys, a second for sorting the temporary table and a third pass to join and compare the records within the window.

Compared to the exhaustive method, the number of comparisons is greatly reduced, namely to $w \cdot n$. If $w < \log n$, the comparisons are dominated by the sorting phase, which requires $O(n \log n)$ comparisons. As opposed to the blocking method, the number of comparisons is accurately predictable.

Research has produced many variants of SNM: Monge and Elkan [1997] adopt the general SNM approach, but propose both a domain-independent similarity measure and the union-find data structure to efficiently manage candidate pairs and detected duplicate groups. It defines a representative of each already detected duplicate group. Records are first compared only to that representative, and thus many comparisons are avoided. Only if similarity to the representative is high enough, does a more complete comparison with all member of the duplicate group commence. An SNM variant for nested XML data is presented by Puhlmann et al. [2006] and described among other algorithms for non-relational data in Section 4.2.1.

4.1.3   COMPARISON

Blocking and Sorted-Neighborhood have much in common. Both aim at reducing the number of comparisons by making intelligent guesses as to which pairs of records have a chance of being duplicates. Both rely on some intrinsic ordering of the data and the assumption that records that are close to each other with respect to that order have a higher chance of being duplicates than other pairs of records. Their closeness is maybe best characterized by the work of Yan et al. [2007] in which they present an "adaptive sorted neighborhood" method, which in fact (and inadvertently?) turns out to be a blocking method. A deeper comparison and a generalization of both methods is presented by Draisbach and Naumann [2009]. Table 4.1 shows the computational complexities of the different methods and compares them to the full enumeration of all pairs of records.

Finally, it has been noted that a more effective way of reducing the search space is to prune entire records, not just pairs. If it can be easily shown for a particular record that its similarity to all other records is below the threshold, all candidate pairs that involve this record can be eliminated. However, checking this condition is not trivial and only applicable in few occasions.

Table 4.1: Complexity analysis with number of partitions b, window size w and number of records n (from Draisbach and Naumann [2009])

	Blocking	Windowing	Full enum.
Number of comparisons	$\frac{1}{2}(\frac{n^2}{b} - n)$	$(w-1)(n - \frac{w}{2})$	$\frac{n^2-n}{2}$
Key generation	$O(n)$	$O(n)$	n/a
Sorting	$O(n \log n)$	$O(n \log n)$	n/a
Detection	$O(n^2/b)$	$O(wn)$	$O(n^2)$
Overall	$O(n\,(n/b + \log n))$	$O(n(w + \log n))$	$O(n^2)$

4.2   ALGORITHMS FOR DATA WITH COMPLEX RELATIONSHIPS

In the previous section, we discussed algorithms that efficiently determine duplicate pairs. They have in common that they classify a pair of candidates as duplicate or non-duplicate solely by using the object description of the two candidates. That is, pairs of candidates are compared and classified independently of other candidates. In Section 2.3, we discussed that for comparisons, we can use relationship descriptions in addition to object descriptions during comparisons.

In this section, we describe algorithms that consider relationships. In Section 4.2.1, we discuss algorithms specialized to hierarchical relationships, including XML data. These algorithms not only use relationship descriptions to potentially improve the effectiveness of duplicate detection, but they also prune pairwise comparisons based on relationships. In Section 4.2.2, we then show how relationships between candidates that result in a graph structure potentially improve effectiveness.

4.2.1   HIERARCHICAL RELATIONSHIPS

All algorithms that exploit hierarchical relationships have in common that they assume that a given candidate type can occur at exactly one level of the hierarchy (although several candidate types may appear on the same level), i.e., all addresses of a customer appear in the same position in a hierarchy, but at that same level, there may also be other data, such as phone numbers.

One possibility to exploit the hierarchical structure is to traverse the tree in a top-down fashion [Ananthakrishna et al., 2002; Weis and Naumann, 2004]. That is, candidates at the topmost level l_1 are compared before we proceed to level l_2 and so on. To prune comparisons, algorithms proceeding in top-down order assume that the parent-child relationships reflect 1:N relationships of the real world. For instance, assume that cities are nested under countries. This nesting reflects a 1:N relationship of the real world, as a city is usually not split over several countries, whereas a country in general has more than one city. Based on the 1:N relationship assumption, it is true that two candidates on level l_{i+1} may only be duplicates if their parents on level l_i are duplicates (or are the same parent). Indeed, it does not make sense to compare cities from different countries. As a consequence, when traversing the data in a top-down fashion, we can prune comparisons based on duplicate classifications previously performed on ancestors.

The SXNM algorithm [Puhlmann et al., 2006] does not assume a 1:N relationship between parent and child elements, and, therefore, does not apply the same pruning principle. Instead, it traverses the hierarchy from bottom to top to, for instance, also detect duplicate authors that are nested under non-duplicate books. Comparisons are pruned using an extension of the Sorted Neighborhood method. When proceeding from level l_i to l_{i-1}, SXNM uses the knowledge of duplicates in children, which are part of the relationship description of candidates on level l_{i-1} to compute similarity, for instance, using one of the specialized XML similarity measures presented in Section 3.4.

4.2.2   RELATIONSHIPS FORMING A GRAPH

As the algorithms on hierarchical data show, relationship descriptions allow us to propagate comparison results from one pairwise comparison to another, related comparison. Indeed, in the top-down traversal, the fact that two candidates are not duplicates is propagated to the child candidates, whereas in SXNM, children similarities are propagated to the parent level.

In the general case, relationships between candidates can form a graph. Therefore, we refer to algorithms performing duplicate detection on such relationship graphs as graph algorithms. In this section, we discuss a general framework for graph algorithms [Weis, 2008] that applies to several algorithms proposed in the literature [Bhattacharya and Getoor, 2007; Dong et al., 2005].

To better illustrate the concepts underlying graph algorithms, we use the following example.

Example 4.1   Relationship graph.   Assume we have candidates of type author, paper, and venue. Relationship descriptions translate the following relationships:

- The set of papers appearing in a venue is descriptive of that venue.

- The set of authors of a paper is descriptive of a paper.

In Figure 4.4(a), we show data for two papers with the associated author and venue information. This data may have been extracted from two services that use different representations of authors and venues. We added labels to uniquely identify publications, authors, and venues. Note that $a3$ is recognized as shared author between both publications because the author name is exactly equal. A sample graph that illustrates how the candidates of Figure 4.4(a) relate to each other based on their relationship descriptions is depicted in Figure 4.4(b). In this graph, an edge points from candidate c_1 to candidate c_2 if c_2 is part of the relationship description of c_1.

In the above example, the relationship description of a candidate of a given type T consists of neighboring candidates in the relationship graph that may help identify duplicates of a candidate of type T. For instance, the relationship description of candidates of type venue consists of papers appearing in that venue. If papers are detected to be duplicates or if they are very similar, then the likelihood increases that their respective venues are duplicates as well. As discussed in Section 2.3.1, defining relationship descriptions requires domain-knowledge, and we assume that a domain expert

Information extracted for a publication P1
$p1$: Duplicate record detection: A survey
$a1$: A.K. Elmagarmid
$a2$: P.G. Ipeirotis
$a3$: V.S. Verykios
$v1$: Transactions on knowledge and data engineering

Information extracted for a publication P2
$p2$: Duplicate Record Detection
$a4$: Elmagarmid
$a3$: P.G. Ipeirotis
$a5$: Verykios
$v1$: TKDE

(a) Sample data

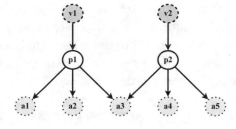

(b) Sample relationship graph

Figure 4.4: Relationships between candidates of type publication (p), author (a), & venue (v)

was able to define dependencies at schema level. That is, the dependency is defined by knowledge of the form "venue candidates depend on paper candidates that are published in that venue".

Based on relationship descriptions defined at schema level, we can determine relationships at instance level to obtain a relationship graph similar to the graph depicted in Figure 4.4(b). Based on this graph, graph algorithms for duplicate detection then generally start with an iterative process that compares (all) pairs of candidates. This iterative phase can be divided into three individual steps, namely the retrieval step, the classification step, and the update step. Before we formally describe the process, we illustrate the general idea by continuing our example from the publications domain.

Example 4.2 Iterative phase of graph algorithms.   Given all candidates depicted in Figure 4.4, we need to classify the following candidate pairs as duplicates or non-duplicates:

$$(v_1, v_2), (p_1, p_2), (a_1, a_2), (a_1, a_3), (a_1, a_4), (a_1, a_5),$$
$$(a_2, a_3), (a_2, a_4), (a_2, a_5), (a_3, a_4), (a_3, a_5), (a_4, a_5)$$

As candidates depend on related candidates in their relationship description, *pairs* of candidates depend on *pairs* of related candidates. For instance, the candidate pair that consists of venues v_1 and v_2 depends on the comparison results of candidate pair (p_1, p_2). Let the pairs be processed in the order listed above. Then, when (v_1, v_2) are compared, we do not have enough evidence that the two venue candidates are duplicates – the strings *Transactions on knowledge and data engineering* and *TKDE* are quite different. However, once authors and papers have been classified as duplicates, we have enough evidence to classify the venues as duplicates too. So, as we compare paper candidates, we propagate their similarities and duplicate classifications to venues and we need to compare venues again.

An interesting fact of all graph algorithms for duplicate detection is that they may compare a pair of candidates more than once, based on additional knowledge gained during related comparisons.

This propagation of similarities or duplicate classifications allows to detect hard cases where object descriptions alone do not suffice to detect duplicates. For instance, no similarity measure based on object descriptions alone is capable of identifying that the venue *TKDE* is the same as *Transactions on knowledge and data engineering*. However, comparing a pair more than once may compromise efficiency. Therefore, different algorithms devise different heuristics to reduce the number of pair-wise comparisons by choosing a "smart" comparison order. For instance, if we change the order of comparisons described in Example 4.2 to

$$(a_1, a_2), (a_1, a_3), (a_1, a_4), (a_1, a_5), (a_2, a_3), (a_2, a_4),$$
$$(a_2, a_5), (a_3, a_4), (a_3, a_5), (a_4, a_5), (p_1, p_2), (v_1, v_2)$$

we can verify that no comparison needs to be performed more than once, even though we propagate similarities. To avoid re-comparisons, the order may need to be updated before the next pair is compared, so we essentially maintain a priority queue that needs to be updated every time information is propagated.

Let us now define the general process of pairwise comparisons in graph algorithms more formally. The input to the iterative phase of graph algorithms is a relationship graph and an initial priority queue PQ that contains all candidate pairs we want to compare. The order of PQ is defined by an algorithm-specific heuristic that aims at avoiding re-comparisons of candidate pairs.

Step 1: Retrieval. Retrieve the first pair in PQ as determined by the heuristic used for ordering.

Step 2: Classification. The retrieved pair of candidates (c, c') is classified using a similarity measure that takes into account both the candidates' object-descriptions and relationship-descriptions, i.e., it uses $OD(c)$, $OD(c')$, $RD(c)$, and $RD(c')$. Appropriate similarity measures are, for instance, adaptations of one of the comparison techniques discussed in Chapter 3. Two classification results are possible: either c and c' are duplicates, or they are classified as non-duplicates. We may decide to propagate these classification results to dependent candidate pairs (d, d') whose relationship descriptions $RD(d)$ and $RD(d')$ contain c and c', respectively. Essentially, this means that we propagate the information "c is a (non-) duplicate of c'" to the parents of c and c' in our graph representation. Alternatively, we may also propagate the information "The similarity between c and c' equals X" and make the actual classification of c and c' later.

Step 3: Update. When a similarity or a duplicate classification needs to be propagated after the comparison of (c, c'), we identify all dependent pairs (d, d') of candidates from PQ where $c \in RD(d)$ and $c' \in RD(d')$. For each such pair, we update any information that is affected by the propagated information (e.g., the overlap between relationship descriptions). Depending on the implementation, the priority queue order is updated to reflect the propagation. In any case, if the pair (d, d') has been classified previously and is therefore no longer present in PQ, we need to add it back to PQ. Overall, the update phase simply updates all necessary information used by the next retrieval and classification steps.

The complexity of the algorithm is $O(n^4)$ in the worst case, where n is the number of candidates of a same type. However, the worst case is highly unlikely in practice because it assumes (i) all n candidates to be compared (without any application of blocking or another pruning technique discussed in Section 4.1), (ii) all pairs of candidates are in fact duplicates, (iii) all pairs of candidates depend on all other pairs, and (iv) the comparison order identifying a duplicate at the last position in PQ so that all previous candidates need to be added back. On average, the complexity is in $O(n^2)$, the same as for non-graph algorithms, so, in general, exploiting relationships between candidates is worth re-comparisons when the goal of the application is high effectiveness.

4.3 CLUSTERING ALGORITHMS

So far, we have discussed algorithms that iteratively detect pairs of duplicates using a similarity-based duplicate classifier (see Chapter 3). As we have seen in Section 4.1, the number of pairwise comparisons can effectively be reduced to a fraction of all possible pairs, yielding satisfactory efficiency while maintaining high effectiveness in terms of pairwise classifications.

However, duplicate pairs are not the final result of duplicate detection. Indeed, the goal is to partition a set of candidates C (of a given type T) into sets of candidates where each set represents a different real-world object and all candidates within such a set are different representations of the same real-world object (Section 2.1). In this section, we discuss two alternatives on how such duplicate clusters can be obtained. The first alternative uses the pairwise classification results obtained by a pairwise algorithm to form duplicate clusters. This alternative is commonly used as a post-processing of pairwise algorithms. The second alternative more seamlessly integrates both the pairwise comparisons and clustering and adjusts to data and cluster characteristics.

4.3.1 CLUSTERING BASED ON THE DUPLICATE PAIR GRAPH

The result of pairwise algorithms can be represented as a graph where nodes represent candidates and edges between candidates exist if the pairwise algorithm considers them to be duplicates (based on a pairwise classification). Edges may also have a weight, that either corresponds to a similarity or a distance score. We refer to such a graph as the *duplicate pair graph*.

Example 4.3 Let us consider the relational data described in Figure 4.5(a). It shows an excerpt of a media database that stores music tracks together with an artist. We also include an id attribute for future reference. Obviously, the correct duplicate clusters are $\{1, 2\}$, $\{3, 4\}$, and $\{9, 10, 11\}$. Using a similarity-based duplicate classification, we might detect duplicate pairs $\{1, 2\}$, $\{3, 4\}$, $\{3, 5\}$, $\{5, 6\}$, $\{6, 7\}$, $\{5, 8\}$, $\{9, 10\}$, $\{9, 11\}$, $\{10, 11\}$, $\{9, 12\}$, $\{10, 12\}$. The corresponding duplicate pair graph is depicted in Figure 4.5(b), where edges are labeled with their weight corresponding to the pairwise similarity score of the two connected candidates.

Based on the duplicate pair graph, the goal now is to determine sets of candidates that actually represent the same real-world object. We describe two directions that have been used in the

id	artist	track
1	Tori Amos	Beekeeper
2	Amos, Tori	Beekeeper
3	Beethoven	Symphony Nr. 5
4	Ludwig van Beethoven	5th Symphony
5	Beethoven	Symphony Nr. 1
6	Beethoven	Symphony Nr. 2
7	Beethoven	Symphony Nr. 3
8	Schubert	Symphony Nr. 1
9	AC DC	Are you ready
10	AC/DC	Are you ready
11	AC/DC	Are U ready
12	Bob Dylan	Are you Ready
13	Michael Jackson	Thriller

(a) Sample data in a media database

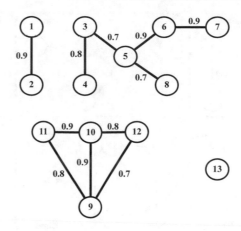

(b) Example for a duplicate pair graph

Figure 4.5: Graph representation of the result of pairwise duplicate detection

literature, namely (i) partitioning based on connected components [Hernández and Stolfo, 1995] and (ii) partitioning based on centers [Hassanzadeh et al., 2009].

Partitioning based on connected components is based on the observation that the relationship "is-duplicate-of" is transitive. Indeed, if we say that the track candidate 3 is a duplicate of both candidate 5 and candidate 4, the semantics of a duplicate relationship, that dictate that duplicates represent the same real-world object, requires candidates 4 and 5 to be duplicates as well. We introduce an edge between two candidates into the duplicate pair graph if and only if he two candidates are duplicates. Then, we can easily determine clusters of duplicates based on the transitivity of the is-duplicate-of relation by computing the transitive closure over the graph in order to partition it into its connected components.

Example 4.4   Consider the duplicate pair graph of Figure 4.5(b). It has four connected components that, using the partitioning method just described, produces four duplicate clusters highlighted in Figure 4.6(a). If we now regard the actual data (Figure 4.5(a)), we see that through long chains of pairwise duplicates, we end up, for instance, with candidates 4 and 8 being duplicates, although their respective object descriptions {(*artist*, *Ludwig van Beethoven*), (*track*, *5th Symphony*)} and {(*artist*, *Schubert*), (*track*, *Symphony Nr. 1*)} barely have anything in common!

The example above illustrates the major drawback of simply computing duplicate clusters as the set of connected components in the duplicate pair graph. To remedy this problem, one solution is to simply revoke duplicate classifications to obtain more (but smaller) connected components. One such edge removal strategy is to recursively remove the edge with the lowest similarity until a satisfactory result is obtained. A satisfactory result may be that we do not have transitivity paths

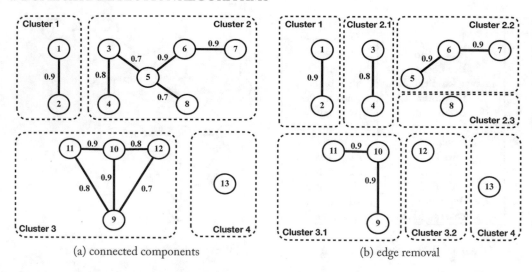

(a) connected components   (b) edge removal

Figure 4.6: Clusters using connected components (a) and edge removal (b)

longer than a certain number of steps, or that the lowest similarity between any two candidates should not fall under a given threshold.

Example 4.5 Consider Cluster 3 of Figure 4.6(a). Edge weights represent similarities, and because we observe that the similarity between candidate 11 and candidate 12 is too low, we decide that we need to remove edges until these two candidates fall into separate components. We remove edges in increasing order of their similarity. The lowest similarity is 0.7 and the corresponding edge connects candidates 9 and 12. Because candidates 11 and 12 are still transitively connected, we continue to remove edges with next lowest similarity, e.g., 0.8. After this step, candidates 11 and 12 are no longer in the same component, so we stop removing edges from Cluster 3, which is now divided into two separate components. We apply the same procedure on Cluster 2 in order to separate components for candidates 4 and 8. The final result is depicted in Figure 4.6(b).

Another method to divide connected components into smaller partitions, which correspond to duplicate clusters, is to determine centers within a connected component and to require that a candidate is part of the cluster of the closest center. To compute centers, we sort the edges of the duplicate pair graph in descending order of their similarity. The algorithm then scans the sorted set of edges and each time a candidate c first occurs in a scanned candidate pair (that corresponds to the source and target candidates of an edge), it is assigned as the center of a duplicate cluster. All edges subsequently scanned and that connect candidate c to another candidate c' are then part of the cluster centered around c so that c' is part of the cluster centered in c. Once c' is assigned a cluster, it is never considered again.

Example 4.6   Consider again Cluster 3 of Figure 4.6(a). When sorting edges in ascending order of their similarity, the first similarity score to be considered in the subsequent scan is 0.9. Assume that edge (11, 10) happens to be scanned first, and that we decide that candidate 11 is the new center. Then 10 is obviously part of the cluster centered at 11. The next edge to be considered is (10, 9). Candidate 10 is already part of a cluster, so we just leave it there. Candidate 9, on the other hand, occurs for the first time, so it is set to be the center of the next cluster. The next edge we scan is (11,9). Both candidates it connects are already part of a cluster. Next, edge (10, 12) is processed, yielding the next center, i.e., candidate 12. We note that all candidates are now part of a cluster with a center, so we can stop the computation. Figure 4.7(a) shows the final result of processing all connected components of Figure 4.6(a) using the center approach. We observe that the initial Cluster 2 is now split into three separate clusters (2.1, 2.2, and 2.3). The same is true for Cluster 3 that is now divided into clusters 3.1, 3.2, and 3.3.

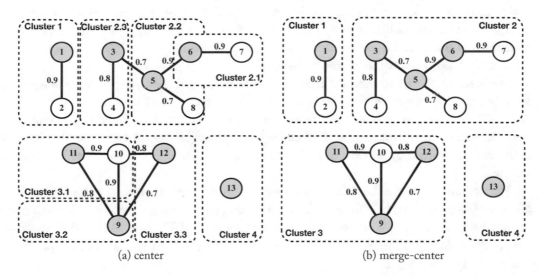

(a) center   (b) merge-center

Figure 4.7: Clusters using center (a) and merge-center (b)

In the example above, we observe that the order of edges with equal similarities and the candidate selected as a center when processing a pair potentially affects the selection of center nodes as well as the final partitioning. Indeed, when processing the first pair (10, 11) of Cluster 3, had we chosen candidate 10 as the center instead of candidate 11, the final result would have been equal to the initial Cluster 3. An extension of the simple center-based algorithm just described that attenuates these effects is to merge two clusters whenever the center of one cluster is similar to the center of the other cluster. A possible final result of this variant, called merge-center, is depicted in Figure 4.7(b).

In this section, we discussed several algorithms that determine duplicate clusters based on a previously computed duplicate pair graph. These methods can be used as a post-processing step after pairwise duplicate classification. Which of these algorithms is best suited highly depends on the application domain, the distribution of duplicates, and how "dirty" these duplicates are. One reason for this is that these approaches are solely based on global thresholds and parameters, and they do not adjust to changing characteristics of the data or the initial clusters formed by pairwise classifications. For instance, using the merge-center algorithm, we see that both Cluster 2 and Cluster 3 remain connected, although the shape of the clusters significantly differs: In Cluster 3, the shortest path from any node to the other is at most 2, whereas in Cluster 2, it varies between 1 and 4. In the next section, we describe an algorithm that integrates both pairwise comparisons and clustering but adjusts to local characteristics of data and clusters to potentially better partition the set of candidates into duplicate clusters.

4.3.2   CLUSTERING ADJUSTING TO DATA & CLUSTER CHARACTERISTICS

The algorithm we present in this section determines duplicate clusters based on the observation that duplicates of a same object usually have a small distance to each other, and they have only a small number of other candidates within a small distance [Chaudhuri et al., 2005]. To capture these properties, the criteria of *compact set* and *sparse neighborhood* are introduced.

We illustrate these two concepts in Figure 4.8. Intuitively, these concepts define two growth spheres: in the inner sphere, which corresponds to the compact set, we find only candidates that are all mutually closest to each other; in second sphere, we find very few candidates that are close to candidates in the inner sphere, thereby forming a sparse neighborhood. Note that the closeness to a candidate is defined by a radius of p times the minimal distance of a candidate to its closest candidate.

We can interpret the radius of each sphere as a threshold that separates duplicates from non-duplicates. However, in contrast to algorithms performing pairwise classifications that use a single fixed threshold, we can have different thresholds for each cluster! This makes the algorithm more robust to the chains of pairwise matches that yield two very dissimilar candidates as duplicates as we observed in Section 4.3.1.

Before we describe the algorithm that determines duplicate clusters based on the compact set and sparse neighborhood properties, we need to define these two concepts more precisely and require some notation. Let us first define a compact set, denoted as CS. Essentially, a set of candidates is a compact set iff for every candidate $c \in CS$, the distance $dist(c, c')$ between c and any other candidate $c' \in CS$ is less than the distance $dist(c, c'')$ between c and any other candidate not part of the compact set. For a candidate c, we define $nn(c)$ as the distance between c and its nearest neighbor within a compact set. The neighborhood $N(c)$ is then defined by a distance of $p \times nn(c)$. The neighborhood growth $ng(c)$ is the number of candidates in the neighborhood $N(c)$ of candidate c. Then, let α be an aggregation function and $k > 0$ be a constant. Intuitively, k is a threshold that

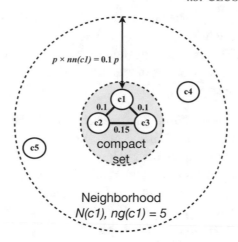

Figure 4.8: Compact set and sparse neighborhood of a candidate c_1

prevents a sparse neighborhood from including too many candidates. We say that a set of records is a sparse neighborhood, denoted as $SN(\alpha, k)$, if (i) $|SN(\alpha, k)| = 1$ or (ii) the aggregated value of neighborhood growths of all candidates within $SN(\alpha, k)$ is less than k.

The clustering algorithm based on these two concepts determines clusters of duplicate candidates such that all clusters satisfy these two properties. It is defined for candidates that correspond to records of a relational table. Formally, given a set of candidates C, a distance function $dist$, an aggregation function α, a positive constant k, and an integer constant I, the goal is to partition C into a minimum number of groups such that each group is a compact set with sparse neighborhood and each group contains at most I candidates. The restriction of the size of a group allows for efficient computation (see discussion on complexity), but more importantly, it avoids the creation of very large groups that encompass two candidates c and c' that are not actual duplicates although c' is among the I most similar candidates to c (and vice versa). Alternatively, we may also use a similarity threshold to define the minimum similarity that has to exist between any two candidates in a group. In the following, we only consider the first variant where the cardinality of a group is limited by I. The problem is solved in a two-phase algorithm, which we briefly describe next.

Phase 1: Nearest-neighbor list computation. The goal of this phase is to determine, for each candidate c, the set of nearest neighbors of c as well as its neighborhood growth. For each candidate c, we thus determine a triple $\langle cid, nnList, ng \rangle$, where cid uniquely identifies candidate c, $nnList$ is a set of nearest neighbors of c, and ng is the neighborhood growth of c. The nearest-neighbor list of c consists of the I closest candidates to c.

The fact that candidates originate from records stored in a relational database allows the use of indices to process queries of the form: given any candidate (record) c, fetch its nearest neighbors. If no indices are available, nested loops join methods are used in this phase.

Phase 2: Partitioning phase. The second phase uses the output of Phase 1 to partition the original set of candidates into a minimum number of groups that correspond to compact sets with sparse neighborhoods. The resulting partitions thus correspond to the final result of duplicate detection. The final result is obtained in two steps, namely the construction step of compact sets and the partitioning step.

Step 1: Compact pair construction. First, we determine if the neighbor sets of varying sizes between 1 and I of two candidates c and c' are equal. Therefore, we compare two candidates c and c' and compute the boolean values $\langle CS_1, CS_2, \ldots, CS_I \rangle$ together with the neighborhood growths $ng(c)$ and $ng(c')$. Essentially, CS_i signifies that the i closest neighbor sets of c and c' are equal. The implementation of this step is based on issuing a SQL query over the output relation of the first phase. This query performs a self-join over the result of Phase 1 and outputs only pairs of candidates (c, c') where the cid of c is smaller than the cid of c' and where c is in $nnList$ of c' and vice versa.

Step 2: Partitioning. Based on the pairs of candidates with equal neighbor sets determined in the previous step, we now determine sets of candidates with neighbor sets that satisfy both the compact set and sparse neighborhood criteria. To achieve this, a query is issued that sorts the results of Step 1 by the cid values of both candidates. Then, each group identified by the cid of c is processed as follows: if c is not already part of another group, we determine the largest subset of the current group such that the aggregate values of the sparse neighborhood of the group is less than the threshold k.

Example 4.7 We illustrate how we may obtain the compact set with sparse neighborhood in Figure 4.9. The result of the first phase is illustrated in Figure 4.9(a), where $nnList$ is sorted in increasing order of the distance of a candidate in $nnList$ to the candidate c identified by cid. In this example, we use $I = 4$, that is, we want to identify compact sets of at most three candidates. Each candidate in the result of Phase 1 is then joined with each other candidate if there exists a compact set of size 3 at most. Such sets are identified by at least one value CS_i being equal to 1. The result of this join, which corresponds to the result of Phase 2, Step 1 is shown in Figure 4.9(b). In a final step, we divide this results into two groups, identified by the value of $cid1$, i.e., the first group corresponds to the first two records in Figure 4.9(b), and the second group corresponds to the third record. We process each group separately: when processing the first group, we place c_1, c_2, and c_3 into a compact set, supposing that the aggregated value of neighborhood growths is below k.

Without appropriate indices, Phase 1 requires a nested loops join, so its complexity is $O(n^2)$, given that n is the size of the candidate set. In Phase 2, we build pairs of candidates and compute compact sets of at most I candidates. That is, every candidate is joined with at most $I - 1$ other candidates, so the complexity is $O(n)$, assuming $I << n$. The size of the output of the first step of Phase 1 is $N < I \times n$. The cost of the second step of Phase 2 is dominated by the cost of sorting

cid	nnList	ng
c_1	$\{c_1, c_2, c_3\}$	3
c_2	$\{c_2, c_1, c_3\}$	3
c_3	$\{c_3, c_1, c_2\}$	3
c_4	$\{c_4, c_3, c_1\}$	3
c_5	$\{c_5, c_2, c_1\}$	3

$(cid1, cid2)$	$\{CS1, CS2, \ldots, CSl\}$	$(ng1, ng2)$
(c_1, c_2)	$\{0, 1, 1\}$	$(3, 3)$
(c_1, c_3)	$\{0, 0, 1\}$	$(3, 3)$
(c_2, c_3)	$\{0, 0, 1\}$	$(3, 3)$

(a) Result of Phase 1   (b) Result of Phase 2, Step 1

Figure 4.9: Clustering based on compact sets with sparse neighborhoods

the output of Step 1, i.e., the cost of Phase 2, Step 1 is $O(N \log N)$. We have seen that N is $O(n)$ so the final cost without indices is

$$O(n^2) + O(n) + O(n \log n) = O(n^2)$$

Using appropriate indices, the complexity may be further reduced to $O(n)$, making this algorithm scalable to large volumes of input data.

CHAPTER 5

Evaluating Detection Success

Measuring the success of duplicate detection is an important but difficult task, usually because of the lack of a gold standard for the data set at hand. Difficulties that prevent a benchmark data set are privacy and confidentiality concerns regarding the data. In this section, we first describe standard measures for success, in particular precision and recall. We then proceed to discuss existing data sets and data generators.

5.1 PRECISION AND RECALL

When detecting duplicates there are two possible types of errors (sometimes referred to as Type I and Type II errors): Candidate pairs that are declared to be duplicate in fact may not be duplicates. We call such errors "false positives". On the other hand, there may be candidate pairs that were not declared to be duplicates while in fact they are. We call such errors "false negatives". In addition, we can distinguish "true positives" – pairs that are correctly declared to be duplicates – and "true negatives" – pairs that are correctly recognized as not being duplicates. In typical scenarios, we expect the latter category to contain the vast majority of candidate pairs.

Figure 5.1 shows these four categories. Among all pairs of records, some are true duplicates and some are declared to be duplicates. It is the goal of duplicate detection algorithms to maximize the intersection between the two. In the following, we assume that we indeed know the cardinalities of the four sets. We discuss, in Section 5.2, the difficulty of obtaining them.

From the cardinalities of the four different sets, one can calculate different success measures for duplicate detection. The most prominent measures are *precision* and *recall*, which are originally defined for information retrieval problems where they reflect the relevance of the document set retrieved by a query. The ultimate goal is to find *only* relevant documents and *all* relevant documents. Intuitively, this corresponds to correctness and completeness of an algorithm. Precision and recall describe how far from that goal a particular solution lies.

For duplicate detection, precision measures the ratio of correctly identified duplicates compared to all declared duplicates, and recall measures the ratio of correctly identified duplicates compared to all true duplicates:

$$\text{precision} = \frac{|\text{true-positives}|}{|\text{true-positives}| + |\text{false-positives}|} = \frac{|\text{true-positives}|}{|\text{declared duplicates}|}$$

$$\text{recall} = \frac{|\text{true-positives}|}{|\text{true-positives}| + |\text{false-negatives}|} = \frac{|\text{true-positives}|}{|\text{true duplicates}|}$$

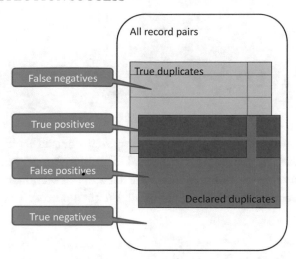

Figure 5.1: Error types in duplicate detection

To understand precision and recall, it is useful to devise algorithms that optimize each measure. To optimize precision, an algorithm can "play safe" and return very few (or no) duplicates. Thus, false positives are avoided leading to high precision. On the downside, this approach minimizes recall because of the high number of false negatives. To maximize recall, an algorithm could declare all n^2 candidate pairs to be duplicates; among them are certainly all true duplicates, but precision suffers immensely.

To find a tradeoff between precision and recall, the F-measure is often used. It is the harmonic mean of precision and recall:

$$\text{F-measure} = \frac{2 \times \text{recall} \times \text{precision}}{\text{recall} + \text{precision}}$$

To understand why the harmonic mean as opposed to the arithmetic mean is the measure of choice, regard Figure 5.2. The left side visualizes on the z-axis the arithmetic mean of the x- and y-axes. Notice the flat surface. The right side of the figure shows the harmonic mean with its distinct curvature. To achieve good F-measure values, both precision and recall must be high. With the typical tradeoff between precision and recall, both must have the same value to maximize the harmonic mean; it does not pay off to achieve especially high values in either. Of course, there are situations in which either precision or recall are of particular importance. For instance, credit-rating agencies must be particularly diligent when detecting customer duplicates, and thus a high precision is of utmost importance, even at the risk of a lower recall [Weis et al., 2008]. The F-measure can also be defined in a weighted fashion [Manning et al., 2008].

To display evaluation results, two types of diagrams are common: the recall-precision diagram and the recall-precision-F-measure diagram. The former plots precision values for increasing recall

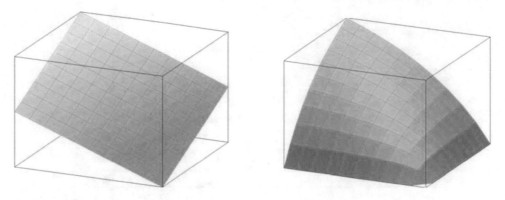

Figure 5.2: Visualization of arithmetic mean (left) and harmonic mean (=F-measure) (right)

– an arbitrarily chosen diagram is shown in Figure 5.3. It can be generated by descendingly sorting all detected pairs by their similarity, ignoring any thresholds, and then analyzing their correctness by decreasing similarity. A typical observation is that precision starts out high, i.e., the most similar pairs are indeed duplicates. For well-chosen similarity measures precision drops sharply at some point. The similarity threshold should be placed at that point.

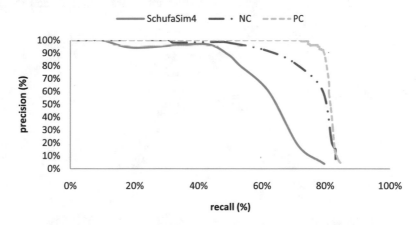

Figure 5.3: A typical recall-precision diagram (based on Weis et al. [2008])

Another way to choose appropriate similarity thresholds is the recall-precision-F-measure diagram. It plots the three measures against increasing (or decreasing) thresholds. The threshold with the highest F-measure can then be chosen for future runs with new data. Figure 5.4 shows such a diagram. Note that precision, recall, and F-measure always meet at the highest F-measure.

In the previous paragraphs, we have examined the tradeoff between precision and recall, which is mainly governed by the similarity threshold. Another tradeoff is the efficiency of the algorithm, i.e., its overall runtime. If a longer runtime is acceptable, more candidate pairs can be compared,

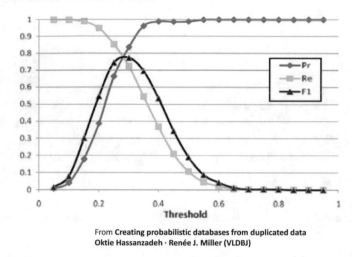

From **Creating probabilistic databases from duplicated data**
Oktie Hassanzadeh · Renée J. Miller (VLDBJ)

Figure 5.4: A typical recall-precision-F-measure diagram (based on Hassanzadeh and Miller [2009])

and thus a higher recall can be achieved. Also, a possibly more elaborate similarity measure can be employed, which increases precision, again at the cost of efficiency. These trade offs are shown in Figure 5.5.

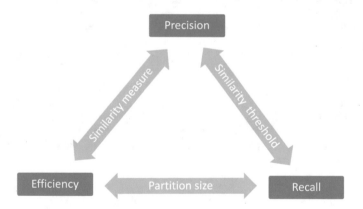

Figure 5.5: Tradeoffs between precision, recall and efficiency

Measuring the efficiency and scalability of duplicate detection is obviously also important; however, since we assume duplicate detection as an offline batch job, it is often not the primary focus of duplicate detection methods. In practice, runtimes of up to a day are usually acceptable for CRM databases with millions of customers. Runtime is measured in the usual way with system timestamps and can be predicted by sampling of smaller data sets. For the online search problem of duplicate detection, again runtime is measured in the usual way. Typically, runtimes must remain under a second and throughput must be sufficiently high.

Duplicate detection is highly parallelizable. In many algorithms, in particular, the pair-wise algorithms of Section 4.1, the decision about a candidate pair is independent of other candidate pairs. Thus, there is a high potential for parallelization, for instance, using the map/reduce paradigm. However, there is not yet much research on this dimension of the problem [Kim and Lee, 2007].

5.2   DATA SETS

All measures mentioned in the previous section assume a known gold-standard, i.e., perfect knowledge of all duplicates in the given data set. In particular, they assume to be able to verify whether a candidate pair is indeed a duplicate (to measure precision), and they assume to know the number of duplicates hidden in the data (to measure recall). In many situations, in particular those where not many duplicates are to be expected, it is possible to manually verify declared duplicates. However, to verify that indeed all duplicates have been detected, theoretically, a manual inspection of all $O(n^2)$ candidate pairs is necessary. For only 10,000 customers, which is the typical number of customers a doctor, car dealership, etc. may have, almost 50 million pairs would have to be inspected manually.

Thus, gold standards are hard to come by. Two alternatives present themselves. First, real-world data sets upon which duplicate detection has previously been executed can provide a baseline, upon which to improve. Second, real-world synthetic data sets can be supplemented with artificially created duplicates.

5.2.1   REAL-WORLD DATA SETS

Real-world data are very valuable to evaluate duplicate detection methods. It is difficult to simulate the types of errors and their distribution as they occur during data entry. On the other hand, real-world data sets in the CRM or product domain are rarely made public due to confidentiality constraints. What is more, customer data by definition include individual-related data and cannot be published even if the data owner would be willing to do so.

A popular data set, used to evaluate duplicate detection in several approaches [Bilenko and Mooney, 2003a; Dong et al., 2005; Singla and Domingos, 2005], is the CORA Citation Matching data set (`http://www.cs.umass.edu/~mccallum/code-data.html`). It lists groups of differently represented references to the same paper. However, this data set is quite small with only 189 unique papers and an average of 9.9 different representations for each.

Another data set, provided by the authors of this lecture and comprises 9,763 records with audio CD information, such as artist, title, and tracks, which were selected randomly from freeDB [Leitão et al., 2007]. In an arduous manual process, involving distributed manual checking and cross-checking of all candidate pairs, a list of 298 true duplicates was detected (`http://www.hpi.uni-potsdam.de/naumann/projekte/repeatability/datasets`).

Other popular real-world data sets include the DBLP data set on papers (`http://dblp.uni-trier.de/xml/`) and the IMDB data set on Movies (`http://www.imdb.com/`

`interfaces`). A repository of other available data sets (both for relational and XML data) and other valuable resources on duplicate detection is the RIDDLE repository (`http://www.cs.utexas.edu/users/ml/riddle/`). However, most data sets require some further processing before they can be used for experiments. For example, the CORA data set includes annotations for duplicate publications but not for authors or venues. When extracting data from IMDB, different sampling techniques (and possibly different error introduction techniques) result in data sets with different characteristics.

Because the gold standard is known for only few of these data sets, researchers have either contaminated the data by inserting duplicates through some automated method (see next section on synthetic data sets), or evaluated only precision. To overcome the problem of determining recall, sampling the data suggests itself; it is certainly easier to examine all pairs of a smaller data set. However, as sampling reduces the number of records, the expected number of duplicates is reduced quadratically: A random 1% sample is expected to contain only 0.01% of the duplicates. For example, from 10,000 original records with 100 (unknown) duplicates, the sample contains 100 records, but only 0.01 duplicate – i.e., probably none.

5.2.2   SYNTHETIC DATA SETS

Synthetic data sets come in two flavors: Contaminated real-world data or generated dirty data. Artificially contaminating a data set provides the knowledge of all duplicates (the gold standard), assuming the data set was clean from the outset. The challenge is to determine how to create duplicates, how many to create (percentage of affected original records, only pairs, or larger size of duplicate groups, etc.), and where to place them within the data set. The following types of data contamination to duplicate records are useful:

- **Exact duplicates.** No change is made to the duplicated object.

- **Missing values.** Remove a subset of the attribute values, replacing them by `NULL` values.

- **Contradictory values.** Change a subset of the values by replacing them with contradictory values, including for example typographical errors, synonyms, abbreviations, or incomplete values. The possibilities here are vast, including swapping of characters, insertion and deletion of random characters, changing capitalization, etc.

To contaminate non-relational data, other types of duplication are possible, such as changing structure or falsifying key references. A tool to generate dirty XML data can be found at `http://www.hpi.uni-potsdam.de/naumann/projekte/dirtyxml`. When contaminating data, even clean data, there is the problem that two duplicated records with different original records might become very similar, possible more similar than to their original records. Such inadvertent duplicates are not recognized as such during the contamination and are thus not part of the gold-standard for that dataset. Note though, that the same problem occurs with real-world data: Two records might be very similar and yet not be duplicates.

In the absence of real-world data, or when it is forbidden to publish, or when characteristics of data should be varied, it is useful to employ so called *data generators*. These usually create data by randomly combining values of existing term lists. These lists contain first names, last names, cities, street names, products, etc. One such generator for CRM data is the UIS Database Generator (`http://www.cs.utexas.edu/users/ml/riddle/data/dbgen.tar.gz`). Others are presented in the SOG project [Talburt et al., 2009] and the ToxGene project [Barbosa et al., 2002]. If frequency distributions are known, these can be used when picking terms for records. For instance, a data generator may generate more addresses in New York City than in Washington D.C. After generating data, it can be contaminated as described above. Again, there is the problem that seemingly duplicates are generated, but they are not recognized as such.

5.2.3   TOWARDS A DUPLICATE DETECTION BENCHMARK

As numerous approaches exist both for increasing efficiency and effectiveness, it is essential to provide some common ground to compare these algorithms with each other. Despite at least a few common data sets, the state-of-the-art does not allow representative comparisons between algorithms yet, for the following main reasons [Weis et al., 2006]:

- **Lack of algorithm documentation.** Many duplicate detection algorithms are described in scientific papers only, and often a 12 page publication cannot cover all details and aspects of an approach. When it comes to re-implementing an existing method, the information provided in a paper is often insufficient.

- **Different testing environments.** When own results are compared to results reported in a paper, the different testing environments may falsify the comparison.

- **Lack of common dataset.** Freely available and simultaneously interesting datasets for duplicate detection are rare. Even more seldom are datasets with true duplicates already marked. As a consequence, even if same or similar datasets were used, the results expressed as precision, recall and runtime measure are not comparable: Two approaches might not agree in what is a correctly detected duplicate and how many duplicates are in fact hidden in the dataset.

- **Obscure methodology.** Comparing results to published results is further problematic because many approaches "fudge" the original data to meet their needs. In papers, we may read sentences like "We further cleaned [a commonly used data set] up by correcting some labels," or "We used the technique [X]" without mentioning how X's tunable parameters are set. In such cases, the methodology is not reproducible, an essential property if we want to compare approaches.

A benchmark for duplicate detection should alleviate the above problems as follows [Weis et al., 2006]:

- **Standardized data.** By applying different duplicate detection approaches on the same data, comparing efficiency or effectiveness of different approaches is easy.

- **Clearly defined operations and metrics.** The problem of lacking documentation about algorithms and experimental methodology is alleviated by defining operations that an algorithm may perform, as well as some clearly defined metrics to evaluate the results of these operations.

- **Central processing.** We envision that the benchmark is executed on a central server to which a duplicate detection algorithm can be submitted, which in turn is executed on the server. This way, the testing environment is guaranteed to be the same across different approaches.

While these goals have not been reached, there are at least some efforts in this direction. The authors of this lecture propose a duplicate detection benchmark with suggestions for data and its contamination, concrete benchmark tasks (the workload), and metrics to fairly evaluate the results [Weis et al., 2006]. Another, similar proposal is by Neiling et al. [2003]. More complex scenarios, e.g., XML duplicate detection or relationship-based duplicate detection, cannot be evaluated using this framework. Finally, Bilenko and Mooney [2003b] present a study on evaluation and training-set construction for adaptive duplicate detection, which is a necessary step towards a benchmark supporting adaptive duplicate detection methods.

CHAPTER 6

Conclusion and Outlook

We conclude this lecture by reiterating the relevance and interestingness but also the difficulty and complexity of the problem of duplicate detection. Duplicates appear in many data sets, from customer records and business transactions to scientific databases and Wikipedia entries. The problem definition – finding multiple representations of the same real world object – is concise, crisp, and clear, but it is comprised of two very difficult problems: Finding an adequate similarity measure to decide upon duplicity and finding an efficient algorithm to detect as many duplicates as possible. This lecture charted the basic state of the art for both problems, suggested use cases, and presented evaluation methods.

Addressing the first problem, that is, finding adequate measures to decide upon the duplicity of records, we discussed several similarity measures and thresholds that allow to decide whether two records are duplicates or not. We distinguished between token-based measures, edit-based measures, and hybrid measures. We have seen that token-based measures are suited in the presence of word swaps or missing words, for instance, in the domain of person names where a middle name might be missing in one record and a first name and last name are swapped. On the other hand, edit-based measures cope well with typographical errors within words. Hybrid measures combine the best of both token-based and edit-based measures. In addition to similarity measures, we saw that domain-knowledge can be used to define rules to identify duplicates and non-duplicates.

A topic not covered in this lecture is the use of machine learning with the goal of tuning similarity measures, thresholds, or weights used to distinguish between duplicates and non-duplicates (Bilenko and Mooney [2003a]; Sarawagi and Bhamidipaty [2002]). Such algorithms are very attractive because they leverage the effort of manual parameter tuning. Using adequate learning models, these approaches outperform the similarity measures discussed in this lecture in terms of the quality of duplicate detection. However, these methods are rarely used in practice because their results are difficult to comprehend and trace and because of the second major problem of duplicate detection, i.e., efficiency.

To improve runtime, numerous algorithms have been proposed. The most widely used class of algorithms is the class of pairwise comparison algorithms. These algorithms compare pairs of records using a suited similarity measure, and their efficiency is improved by saving pairwise comparisons using blocking techniques or the Sorted-Neighborhood method. A class of algorithms that has recently emerged is the class of algorithms that exploit relationships between objects. These algorithms are designed to improve on the quality of the result, but the price to pay is again lower efficiency. Although some approaches explicitly address efficiency in a specialized context, it remains an open issue to design efficient and scalable algorithms for data with complex relationships. Finally, we discussed clustering algorithms. One class of clustering algorithms takes duplicate pairs as input in order to produce sets of records that all represent the same real-world object. A disadvantage of these algorithms is that they require several configuration parameters to be set upfront, and they do not adapt to actual data or cluster characteristics. Therefore, we outlined another clustering algorithm, which adapts to these characteristics.

All algorithms discussed in this lecture compare records to classify them as duplicates. Whenever records have been classified as such, the decision is final and no algorithm considers to revoke these decisions at any point. However, as new data becomes available, new evidence that records are in fact not duplicates may become available, just as non-duplicate records are re-compared when new evidence that they may be duplicates becomes available. An interesting new research direction is to explore how "negative" evidence can be propagated to revoke duplicate decisions and how algorithms that revoke both duplicate decisions and non-duplicate decisions behave. Another line of research is to extend duplicate detection beyond the traditional CRM scenarios. Simple extensions include duplicate detection among companies and products. Detecting duplicate transactions is more difficult due to the intrinsic similarity of many transactions and to the high data volume. Detecting duplicates in streaming data, among text data (near-duplicate web-pages or news articles, plagiarism), among invoices, images, etc. are further and yet mostly unexplored avenues of research.

To conclude, we see that even today, after fifty years of research and development, duplicate detection remains an active field of research and a profitable business case with many companies building software for data cleansing and duplicate detection.

Bibliography

Alexander Albrecht and Felix Naumann. Managing ETL processes. In *Proc. Int. Workshop on New Trends in Information Integration*, pages 12–15, 2008. 5

Rohit Ananthakrishna, Surajit Chaudhuri, and Venkatesh Ganti. Eliminating fuzzy duplicates in data warehouses. In *Proc. 28th Int. Conf. on Very Large Data Bases*, pages 586–597, 2002. DOI: 10.1016/B978-155860869-6/50058-5 34, 43, 48

Denilson Barbosa, Alberto O. Mendelzon, John Keenleyside, and Kelly A. Lyons. ToXgene: a template-based data generator for XML. In *Proc. ACM SIGMOD Int. Conf. on Management of Data*, page 616, 2002. DOI: 10.1145/564691.564769 67

Carlo Batini and Monica Scannapieco. *Data Quality: Concepts, Methods and Techniques*. Springer, 2006. 3

Rohan Baxter, Peter Christen, and Tim Churches. A comparison of fast blocking methods for record linkage. In *Proc. Int. Workshop on Data Cleaning, Record Linkage, and Object Consolidation*, pages 25–27, 2003. 43

Indrajit Bhattacharya and Lise Getoor. Collective entity resolution in relational data. *ACM Trans. Knowl. Discov. Data*, 1(1):Paper 5, 2007. DOI: 10.1145/1217299.1217304 49

Mikhail Bilenko and Raymond J. Mooney. Adaptive duplicate detection using learnable string similarity measures. In *Proc. 9th ACM SIGKDD Int. Conf. on Knowledge Discovery and Data Mining*, pages 39–48, 2003a. DOI: 10.1145/956750.956759 65, 69

Mikhail Bilenko and Raymond J. Mooney. On evaluation and training-set construction for duplicate detection. In *Proc. Int. Workshop on Data Cleaning, Record Linkage, and Object Consolidation*, pages 7–12, 2003b. 68

Mikhail Bilenko, Raymond J. Mooney, William W. Cohen, Pradeep D. Ravikumar, and Stephen E. Fienberg. Adaptive name matching in information integration. *IEEE Intelligent Systems*, 18(5): 16–23, 2003. DOI: 10.1109/MIS.2003.1234765 24

Mikhail Bilenko, Beena Kamath, and Raymond J. Mooney. Adaptive blocking: Learning to scale up record linkage. In *Proc. 2006 IEEE Int. Conf. on Data Mining*, pages 87–96, 2006. DOI: 10.1109/ICDM.2006.13 43

C. Bizer, J. Lehmann, S. A. Georgi Kobilarov, C. Becker, R. Cyganiak, and S. Hellmann. Db-pedia – a crystallization point for the web of data. *J. Web Semantics*, 7(3):154–165, 2009a. DOI: 10.1016/j.websem.2009.07.002 11

Christian Bizer, Tom Heath, and Tim Berners-Lee. Linked data – the story so far. *J. Semantic Web and Information Systems*, 5(3):1–22, 2009b. 10

Jens Bleiholder and Felix Naumann. Data fusion. *ACM Comput. Surv.*, 41(1):Paper 1, 2008. DOI: 10.1145/1456650.1456651 2

Jens Bleiholder, Zoé Lacroix, Hyma Murthy, Felix Naumann, Louiqa Raschid, and Maria-Esther Vidal. BioFast: Challenges in exploring linked life science sources. *ACM SIGMOD Rec.*, 33(2): 72–77, 2004. DOI: 10.1145/1024694.1024706 9

Jens Bleiholder, Sascha Szott, Melanie Herschel, Frank Kaufer, and Felix Naumann. Subsumption and complementation as data fusion operators. In *Advances in Database Technology, Proc. 13th Int. Conf. on Extending Database Technology*, 2010. 8

Charles P. Bourne and Donald F. Ford. A study of methods for systematically abbreviating english words and names. *J. ACM*, 8(4):538–552, 1961. DOI: 10.1145/321088.321094 39

Surajit Chaudhuri, Venkatesh Ganti, and Rajeev Motwani. Robust identification of fuzzy duplicates. In *Proc. 21st Int. Conf. on Data Engineering*, Tokyo, Japan, 2005. DOI: 10.1109/ICDE.2005.125 56

Jens Dittrich, Marcos Antonio Vaz Salles, and Lukas Blunschi. imemex: From search to information integration and back. *Q. Bull. IEEE TC on Data Eng.*, 32(2):28–35, 2009. 10

AnHai Doan, Ying Lu, Yoonkyong Lee, and Jiawei Han. Profile-based object matching for informa-tion integration. *IEEE Intelligent Systems*, 18(5):54–59, 2003. DOI: 10.1109/MIS.2003.1234770 40, 42

Xin Dong and Alon Y. Halevy. A platform for personal information management and integration. In *Proc. 2nd Biennial Conf. on Innovative Data Systems Research*, pages 119–130, 2005. 10

Xin Dong, Alon Halevy, and Jayant Madhavan. Reference reconciliation in complex informa-tion spaces. In *Proc. ACM SIGMOD Int. Conf. on Management of Data*, pages 85–96, 2005. DOI: 10.1145/1066157.1066168 49, 65

Uwe Draisbach and Felix Naumann. A comparison and generalization of blocking and windowing algorithms for duplicate detection. In *Proc. Int. Workshop on Quality in Databases*, pages 51–56, 2009. 47, 48

Ahmed K. Elmagarmid, Panagiotis G. Ipeirotis, and Vassilios S. Verykios. Duplicate record detection: A survey. *IEEE Trans. Knowl. and Data Eng.*, 19(1):1–16, 2007. DOI: 10.1109/TKDE.2007.250581 11

Ivan Fellegi and Alan Sunter. A theory of record linkage. *J. American Statistical Association*, 64(328): 183–1210, 1969. DOI: 10.2307/2286061 2

César A. Galindo-Legaria. Outerjoins as disjunctions. In *Proc. ACM SIGMOD Int. Conf. on Management of Data*, pages 348–358, 1994. DOI: 10.1145/191843.191908 8

Alon Y. Halevy, Michael J. Franklin, and David Maier. Principles of dataspace systems. In *Proc. 25th ACM SIGACT-SIGMOD-SIGART Symp. on Principles of Database Systems*, pages 1–9, 2006. DOI: 10.1145/1142351.1142352 10

Pei Hao, Wei-Zhong He, Yin Huang, Liang-Xiao Ma, Ying Xu, Hong Xi, Chuan Wang, Bo-Shu Liu, Jin-Miao Wang, Yi-Xue Li, and Yang Zhong. MPSS: an integrated database system for surveying a set of proteins. *Bioinformatics*, 21(9):2142 – 2143, 2005. DOI: 10.1093/bioinformatics/bti306 9

Oktie Hassanzadeh and Renée J. Miller. Creating probabilistic databases from duplicated data. *VLDB J.*, 18(5):1141–1166, 2009. DOI: 10.1007/s00778-009-0161-2 64

Oktie Hassanzadeh, Fei Chiang, Renée J. Miller, and Hyun Chul Lee. Framework for evaluating clustering algorithms in duplicate detection. *Proc. 35th Int. Conf. on Very Large Data Bases*, 2(1): 1282–1293, 2009. 53

Mauricio A. Hernández and Salvatore J. Stolfo. The merge/purge problem for large databases. In *Proc. ACM SIGMOD Int. Conf. on Management of Data*, pages 127–138, 1995. DOI: 10.1145/568271.223807 45, 53

Mauricio A. Hernández and Salvatore J. Stolfo. Real-world data is dirty: Data cleansing and the merge/purge problem. *Data Mining and Knowledge Discovery*, 2(1):9–37, 1998. DOI: 10.1023/A:1009761603038 40, 45

Matthew A. Jaro. Advances in record linking methodology as applied to matching the 1985 census of tampa florida. *J. American Statistical Association*, 84(406):414–420, 1989. DOI: 10.2307/2289924 32

Peter D. Karp. A strategy for database interoperation. *J. Computational Biology*, 2(4):573–583, 1996. DOI: 10.1089/cmb.1995.2.573 9

Hung-sik Kim and Dongwon Lee. Parallel linkage. In *Proc. Int. Conf. on Information and Knowledge Management*, pages 283–292, 2007. DOI: 10.1145/1321440.1321482 65

Luís Leitão, Pável Calado, and Melanie Weis. Structure-based inference of XML similarity for fuzzy duplicate detection. In *Proc. Int. Conf. on Information and Knowledge Management*, pages 293–302, 2007. DOI: 10.1145/1321440.1321483 38, 65

Christopher D. Manning, Prabhakar Raghavan, and Hinrich Schütze. *Introduction to Information Retrieval.* Cambridge University Press, 2008. 62

Diego Milano, Monica Scannapieco, and Tiziana Catarci. Structure aware XML object identification. In *Proc. Int. Workshop on Clean Databases*, page Paper 1, 2006. 37

Alvaro E. Monge and Charles P. Elkan. The field matching problem: Algorithms and applications. In *Proc. 2nd Int. Conf. on Knowledge Discovery and Data Mining*, pages 267–270, 1996. 24, 35

Alvaro E. Monge and Charles P. Elkan. An efficient domain-independent algorithm for detecting approximately duplicate database records. In *Proc. ACM SIGMOD Workshop on Research Issues in Data Mining and Knowledge Discovery*, pages 23—29, 1997. 47

Felix Naumann, Johann-Christoph Freytag, and Ulf Leser. Completeness of integrated information sources. *Inf. Syst.*, 29(7):583–615, 2004. DOI: 10.1016/j.is.2003.12.005 4

Gonzalo Navarro. A guided tour to approximate string matching. *ACM Comput. Surv.*, 33(1):31–88, 2001. DOI: 10.1145/375360.375365 30

Mattis Neiling, Steffen Jurk, Hans-J. Lenz, and Felix Naumann. Object identification quality. In *Proc. Int. Workshop on Data Quality in Cooperative Information Systsems*, 2003. 68

Sven Puhlmann, Melanie Weis, and Felix Naumann. XML duplicate detection using sorted neigborhoods. In *Advances in Database Technology, Proc. 10th Int. Conf. on Extending Database Technology*, pages 773–791, 2006. DOI: 10.1007/11687238_46 47, 49

Erhard Rahm and Philip A. Bernstein. A survey of approaches to automatic schema matching. *VLDB J.*, 10(4):334–350, 2001. DOI: 10.1007/s007780100057 10

Jun Rao, Hamid Pirahesh, and Calisto Zuzarte. Canonical abstraction for outerjoin optimization. In *Proc. ACM SIGMOD Int. Conf. on Management of Data*, pages 671–682, 2004. DOI: 10.1145/1007568.1007643 8

Sunita Sarawagi and Anuradha Bhamidipaty. Interactive deduplication using active learning. In *Proc. 8th ACM SIGKDD Int. Conf. on Knowledge Discovery and Data Mining*, pages 269–278, 2002. DOI: 10.1145/775047.775087 69

Dennis Shasha, Jason Tsong-Li Wang, Kaizhong Zhang, and Shih Frank Y. Exact and approximate algorithms for unordered tree matching. *IEEE Trans. Systems, Man, and Cybernetics*, 24(4):668–678, 1994. DOI: 10.1109/21.286387 39

E. Patrick Shironoshita, Ray M. Bradley, Yves R. Jean-Mary, Thomas J. Taylor, Michael T. Ryan, and Mansur R. Kabuka. Semantic representation and querying of caBIG data services. In *Proc. Int. Workshop on Data Integration for the Life Sciences*, pages 108–115, 2008. DOI: 10.1007/978-3-540-69828-9_10 9

Parag Singla and Pedro Domingos. Object identification with attribute-mediated dependences. In *Principles of Data Mining and Knowledge Discovery, 9th European Conf.*, pages 297–308, 2005. DOI: 10.1007/11564126_31 65

Temple F. Smith and Michael S. Waterman. Identification of common molecular subsequences. *J. Molecular Biology*, 147(1):195–197, 2001. DOI: 10.1016/0022-2836(81)90087-5 31

Lincoln D. Stein. Integrating biological databases. *Nature Reviews Genetics*, 4(5):337 – 345, 2003. DOI: 10.1038/nrg1065 9

John Talburt, Yinle Zhou, and Savitha Shivaiah. SOG: A synthetic occupancy generator to support entity resolution instruction and research. In *Proc. Int. Conf. on Information Quality*, 2009. 67

Giri Kumar Tayi and Donald P. Ballou. Examining data quality. *Commun. ACM*, 41(2):54–57, 1998. DOI: 10.1145/269012.269021 3

Silke Trißl, Kristian Rother, Heiko Müller, Thomas Steinke, Ina Koch, Robert Preissner, Cornelius Frömmel, and Ulf Leser. Columba: an integrated database of proteins, structures, and annotations. *BMC Bioinformatics*, 6:Paper 81, 2005. DOI: 10.1186/1471-2105-6-81 9

Richard Y. Wang and Diane M. Strong. Beyond accuracy: What data quality means to data consumers. *J. Manage. Information Syst.*, 12(4):5–34, 1996. 3

Michael S. Waterman, Temple F. Smith, and W. A. Beyer. Some biological sequence metrics. *Adv. Mathematics*, 20(3):367–387, 1976. DOI: 10.1016/0001-8708(76)90202-4 32

Melanie Weis. *Duplicate Detection in XML Data*. WiKu-Verlag fuer Wissenschaft und Kultur, 2008. 37, 49

Melanie Weis and Felix Naumann. Detecting duplicate objects in XML documents. In *Proc. Int. Workshop on Information Quality for Information Systems*, pages 10–19, 2004. DOI: 10.1145/1012453.1012456 48

Melanie Weis and Felix Naumann. DogmatiX tracks down duplicates in XML. In *Proc. ACM SIG-MOD Int. Conf. on Management of Data*, pages 431–442, 2005. DOI: 10.1145/1066157.1066207 34, 38

Melanie Weis, Felix Naumann, and Franziska Brosy. A duplicate detection benchmark for XML (and relational) data. In *Proc. Int. Workshop on Information Quality for Information Systems*, 2006. 67, 68

Melanie Weis, Felix Naumann, Ulrich Jehle, Jens Lufter, and Holger Schuster. Industry-scale duplicate detection. *Proc. 34th Int. Conf. on Very Large Data Bases*, 1(2):1253–1264, 2008. DOI: http://doi.acm.org/10.1145/1454159.1454165 40, 42, 62, 63

William E. Winkler and Yves Thiboudeau. An application of the Felligi Sunter model of record linkage to the 1990 US decennial census. Technical report, US Bureau of the Census, 1991. 33

Su Yan, Dongwon Lee, Min-Yen Kan, and C. Lee Giles. Adaptive sorted neighborhood methods for efficient record linkage. In *Proc. ACM/IEEE Joint Conf. on Digital Libraries*, pages 185–194, 2007. DOI: 10.1145/1255175.1255213 47

Authors' Biographies

FELIX NAUMANN

Felix Naumann studied mathematics, economy, and computer sciences at the University of Technology in Berlin. After receiving his diploma in 1997 he joined the graduate school "Distributed Information Systems" at Humboldt University of Berlin. He completed his Ph.D. thesis on "Quality-driven Query Answering" in 2000. In 2001 and 2002 he worked at the IBM Almaden Research Center on topics around data integration. From 2003–2006 he was assistant professor for information integration at the Humboldt University of Berlin. Since 2006 he holds the chair for information systems at the Hasso Plattner Institute at the University of Potsdam in Germany. Felix Naumann has published numerous articles in the data quality and data cleansing area, has given tutorials and invited talks on the topic, and has chaired and organized workshops and conferences on data quality.

MELANIE HERSCHEL

Melanie Herschel finished her studies of information technology at the University of Cooperative Education in Stuttgart in 2003. She then joined the data integration group at the Humboldt University of Berlin (2003–2006), and continued her research on data cleansing and data integration at the Hasso Plattner Institute at the University of Potsdam in Germany (2006–2008). She completed her Ph.D. thesis on "Duplicate Detection in XML Data" in 2007. In 2008, she worked at the IBM Almaden Research Center, concentrating her research on data provenance. Since 2009, she pursues research on data provenance and query analysis at the database systems group at the University of Tübingen in Germany. Besides her publications and invited talks on duplicate detection and data cleansing, Melanie Herschel has also been a member of several program committees and has chaired and organized a workshop on data quality.